# AUSTRALIA TRAVEL GUIDE 2023

*The Ultimate Guide to Discovering the Best Places to Visit, Things to Do, and Must-Try Australia Experiences.*

*(Essential Travel Guide)*

**Walden Caldwell**

All rights reserved. No part of this publication may be reproduced, distributed, or transmitted in any form or by any means, including photocopying, recording, or other electronic or mechanical methods, without the prior written permission of the publisher, except in the case of brief quotations embodied in critical reviews and certain other noncommercial uses permitted by copyright law.

Copyright © Walden Caldwell, 2023.

## Table of Contents

Chapter 1: Introduction

    Geography and Climate

    Tips on language, currency, and customs

    The ideal time to visit

Chapter 2: Accommodations

    Top Hotels in Australia

Chapter 3: Transportation

    Options for getting around Australia, including public transportation, taxis, rental cars, and tours

Chapter 4: Food and Drink

    Overview of Australian cuisine and dining options, including recommended restaurants and local specialties

    Tips on finding the best food and drink experiences, such as local markets, food tours, and cooking classes

Chapter 5: Activities and Attractions

> Overview of the top things to do and see in Australia, including museums, landmarks, outdoor activities, and cultural experiences

> Tips on finding the best activities and attractions, such as guided tours and off-the-beaten-path experiences

Chapter 6: Special Events and Festivals

> Communities to Know

> Best Museums and Art Galleries

Chapter 7: Traveling with kids and families

> Kid-friendly attractions and activities

Chapter 8: LGBTQ+ travel - suggestions for LGBTQ+ travelers, including accommodation, nightlife, and events.

Chapter 9: Shopping

> Tips for Making the Most of Your Shopping Experience

> Overview of the local shopping scene in Australia, including markets, boutiques,

and souvenir shops

Tips on finding the best deals, haggling, and shopping locally

Chapter 10: Nightlife in Australia

Overview of the local nightlife scene in Australia, including bars, clubs, and live music venues

Tips on finding the best places to go out, including recommendations for local bands and DJs

Chapter 11: Practical Information

Tips on staying safe and healthy while traveling in Australia , including information on local laws and customs, medical facilities, and emergency resources

Information on visas, travel insurance, and other practical matters

Respecting the local culture and environment

Staying safe and healthy

Common Scams to Avoid

Dealing with unexpected situations

Chapter 12: Itineraries

Suggested itineraries for different lengths of stay and interests, including options for solo travelers, families, and couples.

The thing you should not miss

Making the most of your trip

Final thoughts and next steps

Most frequently asked questions and answers about visiting Australia

Australia Survival Phrases

..... As I boarded my plane to Australia, I couldn't help but feel a mixture of excitement and nerves. I had read Walden Caldwell's Australia Travel Guide cover to cover, and while it had provided me with a wealth of knowledge about the country, I still felt a bit apprehensive about what lay ahead.

But as soon as I stepped off the plane and breathed in the fresh, salty air of Sydney, all my fears melted away. The sun was shining bright and the sky was a deep, crystal blue. I could hear the sounds of seagulls and feel the warm breeze on my face. It was like stepping into a dream.

I took a taxi straight to my hotel in the heart of the city. The hustle and bustle of Sydney's streets was invigorating, and I was eager to explore. I spent my first day wandering around the city, taking in the stunning architecture of the Opera House and Harbor Bridge, and sampling the delicious local cuisine at the famous Sydney Fish Market.

Over the next few days, I continued to explore the city, taking in all the must-see sights like the Royal Botanic Garden, the Australian Museum, and the bustling nightlife of Kings Cross. I also took a day trip to the stunning Blue Mountains, where I was blown away by the sheer natural beauty of the area. As Caldwell had promised, the views were breathtaking, and I felt like I was on top of the world.

Next on my itinerary was the coastal town of Byron Bay. I had read in Caldwell's guide that this was a must-visit destination for anyone who loves the beach, and I was not disappointed. The golden sand beaches, clear blue waters, and relaxed vibe of the town were exactly what I needed to unwind and recharge.

While in Byron Bay, I also took a surfing lesson, something I had always wanted to try. With the help of my patient and experienced instructor, I was able to catch a few waves and experience the thrill of riding the waves.

From there, I traveled up the east coast of Australia, stopping at Cairns, Port Douglas, and the Whitsunday Islands. Each destination was more beautiful than the last, and I couldn't believe how lucky I was to be experiencing it all firsthand.

One of the highlights of my trip was taking a snorkeling tour of the Great Barrier Reef. I had read in Caldwell's guide that this was one of the most beautiful and diverse underwater ecosystems in the world, and I was not disappointed. The colors and diversity of the fish and coral were simply mesmerizing, and I felt like I was swimming in a living, breathing work of art.

As my trip came to a close, I reflected on everything I had experienced and learned during my time in Australia. Caldwell's guide had been an invaluable resource, providing me with insights and recommendations that I would have never discovered on my own.

But it was more than just the practical advice that had made my trip so special. It was the people I had met along the way, the natural beauty of the landscapes, and the sense of adventure and freedom that came with exploring a new and exciting place.

Australia had captured my heart in a way I never thought possible, and I knew that I would always carry a piece of it with me wherever I went. From the stunning landscapes to the friendly people, from the vibrant cities to the quiet countryside, Australia had left an indelible mark on my soul, and I knew that I would be back someday, to experience its magic all over again.

**Kimberly Crain.**

# Chapter 1: Introduction

Australia is a land of endless possibilities, offering an abundance of diverse experiences for first-time visitors. From the stunning coastline to the rugged Outback, Australia is a country that captivates and enchants visitors from all over the world. With its unique flora and fauna, friendly people, and multicultural cities, Australia is a destination that promises to leave a lasting impression.

Australia is the world's sixth-largest country, spanning over 7.6 million square kilometers. The country is divided into six states and two territories, each with its own unique attractions and experiences. New South Wales is home to the iconic Sydney Opera House and Harbour Bridge, while Victoria is renowned for its art, culture, and world-class food scene. Queensland offers some of the best beaches in Australia, and Western Australia boasts stunning natural landscapes, including the famous Kimberley region.

Australia's climate varies from region to region, with tropical climates in the north, arid climates in the interior, and temperate climates in the south. The best time to visit Australia depends on your itinerary and interests. Summer (December to February) is the peak tourist season, with warm weather and long days perfect for beach activities and outdoor adventures. Autumn (March to May) is an excellent time to visit for wine tours and festivals. Winter (June to

August) offers skiing and snowboarding opportunities in the southern states, while spring (September to November) is perfect for hiking and exploring the countryside.

Australia is home to a rich and diverse Indigenous culture, with over 500 Indigenous groups and languages spoken across the country. Visitors can learn about the Indigenous culture through guided tours, cultural centers, and art galleries. Australia also has a multicultural population, with people from all over the world calling Australia home. This diversity is reflected in Australia's cuisine, with a range of international restaurants and food markets to explore.

One of the highlights of visiting Australia is the country's unique wildlife. From kangaroos and wallabies to koalas and wombats, visitors can encounter these iconic animals in their natural habitats. The Great Barrier Reef, one of the seven natural wonders of the world, is also a must-see for visitors. The reef is home to an array of colorful fish, turtles, and other marine life.

Getting around Australia can be challenging, especially if you're planning to explore the country's remote areas. However, Australia has an extensive transport network, including domestic flights, buses, trains, and car rentals. Many visitors choose to hire a camper van or motorhome, allowing them to explore the country at their own pace.

Australia is a safe and welcoming country, with friendly locals and a relaxed way of life. Visitors should be aware of the country's unique natural environment, including bushfires and tropical cyclones, and take appropriate precautions. It's also essential to respect the country's Indigenous culture and customs.

In summary, Australia is a country of contrasts, offering visitors a unique blend of natural beauty, cultural diversity, and adventure. Whether you're exploring the country's vibrant cities or immersing yourself in its stunning natural landscapes, Australia promises to be a destination that will leave a lasting impression. This Australia Travel Guide 2023 is your ultimate resource for planning your perfect trip to Australia, offering practical advice, insider tips, and vivid descriptions to help you make the most of your visit.

## Overview of Australia's History and Culture

Welcome to Australia, a country with a rich and diverse history and culture. As a first-time visitor, it is important to understand the country's past and present to fully appreciate its people, traditions, and values. This overview will provide an insight into the history and culture of Australia, from its ancient Aboriginal roots to its modern multicultural society.

Pre-European Contact

Australia is home to one of the oldest continuous cultures in the world, with the Indigenous people of Australia, the Aboriginal and Torres Strait Islander peoples, having lived on the land for at least 60,000 years. Prior to European settlement, over 250 distinct Indigenous language groups existed across the continent, each with their own unique cultural practices and traditions.

Indigenous Australians had a deep spiritual connection to the land, and their knowledge of the natural environment allowed them to thrive in some of the harshest conditions on earth. They had complex systems of social organization, with family and clan structures that governed their societies.

European Settlement

In 1770, Captain James Cook claimed Australia for Britain, leading to a wave of British settlement in the late 18th and early 19th centuries. The British saw Australia as a new frontier, and a place to send their convicts, who made up the bulk of the early settlers.

The arrival of the British had a devastating impact on Indigenous Australians. They were dispossessed of their land and resources, and subjected to violence, disease, and forced removal from their families. The impact of colonisation is still felt today, with Indigenous Australians experiencing significant disadvantage in areas such as health, education, and employment.

Australian Federation

In 1901, Australia federated to become a single nation, with the six British colonies joining together to form the Commonwealth of Australia. This was a significant moment in Australian history, as it marked the end of British colonial rule and the beginning of an independent Australian nation.

Despite this newfound independence, Australia remained closely tied to Britain for much of the 20th century. It fought alongside Britain in both World Wars, and its political and cultural institutions were heavily influenced by British models.

## Multiculturalism

In the years following World War II, Australia experienced a significant wave of migration, with large numbers of people coming from Europe, Asia, and the Middle East. This has led to the development of a multicultural society, with a diverse range of languages, religions, and cultural practices now present in Australia.

Today, almost half of all Australians were born overseas or have at least one parent who was born overseas. This has had a significant impact on Australian culture, with food, music, art, and fashion from all over the world now part of the national identity.

Sport

Sport is an important part of Australian culture, and has played a significant role in shaping the nation's identity. Australians are passionate about sports such as cricket, rugby, Australian Rules football, and soccer, and many of the country's most famous sporting moments have become part of the national mythology.

The beaches and coastlines of Australia are also popular for water sports such as surfing, swimming, and sailing. Australians take great pride in their sporting achievements, and international events such as the Olympic Games and the Commonwealth Games are eagerly anticipated.

Arts and Literature

Australia has a vibrant arts scene, with a rich tradition of literature, music, and visual arts. Australian writers such as Patrick White, Tim Winton, and Peter Carey have won international acclaim, while musicians such as AC/DC, INXS, and Sia have achieved global success.

Indigenous Australian art is also a significant part of the nation's cultural heritage, with a distinctive style that reflects the ancient traditions and spiritual beliefs of the Indigenous people.

Food and Drink

Australian cuisine has been heavily influenced by the country's multicultural heritage, with a diverse range of dishes now popular across the country. Some of the most iconic Australian foods include meat pies, sausage rolls, Vegemite (a spread made from yeast extract), and the popular snack food, Tim Tams.

Australia is also known for its world-class wines, particularly those produced in the wine regions of South Australia, Victoria, and New South Wales. Australian beer, such as Victoria Bitter and Carlton Draught, is also popular among locals.

National Holidays

Australia celebrates a number of national holidays throughout the year, each with their own significance and traditions. Some of the most important holidays include:

- Australia Day (January 26th) - a celebration of the arrival of the First Fleet and the founding of modern Australia.
- ANZAC Day (April 25th) - a day to commemorate the soldiers who served

in the Australian and New Zealand Army Corps in World War I.
- Christmas Day (December 25th) - a traditional Christian holiday celebrated with family gatherings, gift-giving, and festive meals.
- Boxing Day (December 26th) - a day for sports events and shopping sales.

Australia is a country with a rich and complex history and culture, shaped by its Indigenous roots, British colonialism, and multicultural diversity. As a first-time visitor, it is important to appreciate and respect the diverse traditions and values that make up this unique and dynamic nation. Whether it's exploring the ancient sites of Indigenous Australia, cheering on a local sports team, or indulging in some delicious Aussie cuisine, there is something for everyone to enjoy in this incredible country.

## Geography and Climate

Australia, a country with a vast and diverse landscape, ranging from deserts to rainforests, mountains to beaches. As a first-time visitor, it is important to understand the geography and climate of the country to plan your trip accordingly and make the most of your visit. This overview will provide an insight into the geography and climate of Australia, from its diverse landforms to its variable climate patterns.

### Geography

Australia is the world's sixth-largest country, with an area of approximately 7.6 million square kilometres. It is surrounded by the Pacific and Indian Oceans and is located between the continents of Asia and Antarctica.

The mainland of Australia is divided into six states and two territories, each with its own unique geography and landscape. The states are New South Wales, Queensland, South Australia, Tasmania, Victoria, and Western Australia, while the territories are the Australian Capital Territory and the Northern Territory.

**Landforms**

Australia is known for its vast and diverse landscapes, ranging from deserts to rainforests, mountains to beaches. Some of the most iconic landforms in Australia include:

- The Great Barrier Reef - the world's largest coral reef system, located off the coast of Queensland.
- Uluru (Ayers Rock) - a massive sandstone monolith located in the heart of Australia's Red Centre.
- The Australian Alps - a mountain range that stretches across the southeastern part of the country.

- The Great Dividing Range - a series of mountain ranges that run along the eastern coast of Australia.
- The Outback - a vast, arid region that covers much of the interior of the country.

**Climate**

Australia's climate is variable, ranging from tropical in the north to temperate in the south. The country's location in the southern hemisphere means that its seasons are the opposite of those in the northern hemisphere.

Summer in Australia runs from December to February, while winter runs from June to August. Spring and autumn are typically mild, with temperatures ranging from around 15-25 degrees Celsius.

The climate of Australia is influenced by a number of factors, including its latitude, ocean currents, and prevailing winds. Some of the key climate zones in Australia include:

- Tropical - this climate zone is found in the far north of Australia and is characterized by high temperatures and high humidity.
- Desert - the vast arid regions of central Australia are known for their hot, dry weather and low rainfall.
- Temperate - the southern parts of Australia, including Melbourne, Sydney, and Adelaide, have a temperate climate, with mild temperatures and moderate rainfall.
- Mediterranean - the southwestern corner of Australia, including Perth,

has a Mediterranean climate, with hot, dry summers and cool, wet winters.

**Extreme Weather Events**

Australia is known for its extreme weather events, including bushfires, floods, and cyclones. These events can have a significant impact on the country's infrastructure, economy, and environment.

Bushfires are a major concern in Australia, particularly during the summer months. The country's dry climate and vegetation make it highly susceptible to wildfires, which can cause widespread damage to homes, businesses, and natural habitats.

Floods are also a common occurrence in Australia, particularly in the tropical north and along the eastern coast. Cyclones, which are intense tropical storms, can cause significant damage to coastal regions, with high winds and heavy rainfall leading to flooding and landslides.

Australia's vast and diverse geography, combined with its variable climate patterns, make it an incredible destination for visitors from around the world. Whether you're exploring the ancient landscapes of the Red Centre, snorkeling on the Great Barrier Reef, or hiking through the Australian Alps, there is something for everyone to enjoy in this incredible country. However, it's important to be aware of the potential risks associated with extreme weather events

## Tips on language, currency, and customs

As a first-time visitor to Australia, it's important to be aware of the country's customs and traditions, as well as its language and currency. This guide will provide an overview of some useful tips on language, currency, and customs to help you navigate your way through the country and make the most of your visit.

**Language**

English is the official language of Australia, and is spoken by the majority of the population. However, Australian English has its own unique accent, vocabulary, and grammar, which can take some getting used to for visitors from other English-speaking countries.

Here are some useful tips for navigating the language in Australia:

- Learn some common Australian slang - Australian English has a number of unique slang terms that may be unfamiliar to visitors. Some common examples include "arvo" (afternoon), "brekkie" (breakfast), and "fair dinkum" (true).
- Don't be afraid to ask for clarification - if you're unsure about the meaning of a word or phrase, don't be afraid to

ask for clarification. Australians are generally friendly and helpful, and will be happy to explain any confusing language.
- Be aware of regional accents - Australian accents can vary depending on the region, so it's important to be aware of any differences in pronunciation or vocabulary when traveling to different parts of the country.

**Currency**

The currency used in Australia is the Australian dollar (AUD), which is divided into 100 cents. Banknotes come in denominations of $5, $10, $20, $50, and $100, while coins come in denominations of 5c, 10c, 20c, 50c, $1, and $2.

Here are some useful tips for dealing with currency in Australia:

- Exchange currency before you arrive - if you're coming from overseas, it's a

good idea to exchange some currency before you arrive in Australia, so you have some cash on hand for immediate expenses.
- Use ATMs for currency exchange - ATMs are widely available in Australia, and can be used to withdraw cash in Australian dollars using your foreign debit or credit card.
- Be aware of transaction fees - some banks and ATMs may charge transaction fees for currency exchange, so it's important to be aware of these costs before making any withdrawals.

**Customs**

Australia has a unique set of customs and traditions, which reflect its multicultural heritage and Indigenous roots. Here are some useful tips for navigating customs in Australia:

- Be respectful of Indigenous culture - Australia has a rich Indigenous history, and it's important to be respectful of Indigenous customs and traditions. This includes respecting sacred sites, observing local customs, and being mindful of cultural sensitivities.
- Follow local laws and regulations - Australia has strict laws and regulations, particularly around alcohol, drugs, and tobacco. It's important to be aware of these laws and regulations, and to follow them at all times.
- Be mindful of tipping - tipping is not a common practice in Australia, and is generally not expected in restaurants, cafes, or bars. However, it's always appreciated if you receive exceptional service.

Navigating language, currency, and customs in Australia can be challenging for first-time visitors. However, by being mindful of these tips, you can ensure a more enjoyable and stress-free experience in this incredible country. Whether it's learning some common Aussie slang, exchanging currency, or respecting Indigenous culture, there are plenty of ways to show your appreciation for this unique and dynamic nation.

## **The ideal time to visit**

Australia is a vast and diverse country, with a range of climates and weather patterns depending on the region. This means that the ideal time to visit Australia can vary depending on your interests and the activities you plan to do during your trip. In this guide, we'll explore the best times to visit Australia, based on climate, events, and popular tourist destinations.

Spring (September - November)

Spring is a beautiful time to visit Australia, as the weather is mild and pleasant in many parts of the country. Temperatures range from around 20-25 degrees Celsius (68-77 degrees Fahrenheit) in most regions, making it an ideal time for outdoor activities such as hiking, cycling, and sightseeing.

Some popular destinations to visit in spring include:

- Sydney: Spring is a great time to visit Sydney, as the city comes alive with festivals and events. The Sydney Fringe Festival, the Sydney International Food Festival, and the Good Food Month are just a few of the events that take place during this time.

- Melbourne: Spring is also a great time to visit Melbourne, as the city is known for its vibrant arts and cultural scene. The Melbourne Fringe Festival, the Melbourne Festival, and the Melbourne Cup are just a few of the events that take place during this time.
- Great Barrier Reef: Spring is an ideal time to visit the Great Barrier Reef, as the water temperature is warm and comfortable for swimming and snorkeling. It's also the start of the whale watching season, so you may have the chance to spot humpback whales as they migrate along the coast.

Summer (December - February)

Summer is the peak tourist season in Australia, as many visitors flock to the country to enjoy the warm weather and outdoor activities. Temperatures can soar to over 40 degrees Celsius (104 degrees Fahrenheit) in some regions, so it's important to take precautions against the heat and sun.

Some popular destinations to visit in summer include:

- Beaches: Australia has some of the world's most beautiful beaches, and summer is the perfect time to enjoy them. Some of the most popular beach destinations include Bondi Beach in Sydney, Surfers Paradise on the Gold Coast, and Byron Bay in New South Wales.
- Uluru: Summer is a great time to visit Uluru (also known as Ayers Rock), as the weather is warm and dry. You can take guided tours to explore the area, or simply relax and enjoy the stunning natural scenery.
- Festivals: Summer is also a great time to attend festivals and events in Australia, such as the Sydney New Year's Eve fireworks, the Australian Open tennis tournament in

Melbourne, and the Big Day Out music festival.

Autumn (March - May)

Autumn is a great time to visit Australia, as the weather is mild and comfortable in many regions. Temperatures range from around 15-25 degrees Celsius (59-77 degrees Fahrenheit), making it an ideal time for outdoor activities such as hiking, camping, and sightseeing.

Some popular destinations to visit in autumn include:

- Tasmania: Autumn is a great time to visit Tasmania, as the weather is cool and comfortable for outdoor activities such as hiking and exploring the wilderness areas. The changing colors of the foliage also make for stunning scenery.
- Canberra: Autumn is also a great time to visit Canberra, the capital of Australia, as the city comes alive with

colorful foliage and a range of events and festivals.
- Wine regions: Autumn is the start of the grape harvest season in many of Australia's wine regions, making it a great time to visit and explore the vineyards and wineries.

Winter (June - August)

Winter is the off-season in many parts of Australia, as temperatures can drop below freezing in some regions. However, there are still plenty of reasons to visit Australia during the winter months.

Here are some more details on what you can expect during the winter season in Australia:

Climate and Weather

Winter in Australia runs from June to August, and while the weather can vary depending on the region, it is generally cooler and drier than other seasons. In the southern parts of the country, temperatures can drop to below freezing at night, while daytime temperatures can range from 10-20°C (50-68°F). In the northern regions, temperatures are milder, with daytime temperatures averaging around 25°C (77°F) and nighttime temperatures dropping to around 15°C (59°F).

Activities and Attractions

While the weather may be cooler, there are still plenty of activities and attractions to enjoy during the winter season in Australia. Some popular activities include:

- Skiing and Snowboarding: As mentioned earlier, Australia has a number of ski resorts located in the Snowy Mountains and the Victorian Alps, which offer a range of slopes and trails for skiers and snowboarders of all levels.
- Whale Watching: Winter is the prime time to spot humpback and southern

right whales along the coast of Australia, as they migrate north to warmer waters to breed and give birth. Popular whale watching destinations include Hervey Bay in Queensland, Albany in Western Australia, and the Great Ocean Road in Victoria.
- Hot Air Ballooning: Hot air ballooning is a popular activity in Australia year-round, but the cooler temperatures and clear skies of winter make it an ideal time to take to the skies. Popular destinations for hot air ballooning include the Yarra Valley in Victoria, the Hunter Valley in New South Wales, and the Barossa Valley in South Australia.
- Wine Tasting: Australia has a number of world-renowned wine regions, including the Barossa Valley, Margaret River, and the Hunter Valley. Winter is an ideal time to explore these regions and enjoy a glass of red wine by the fire.

- National Parks: Australia has a number of national parks that offer stunning landscapes and wildlife viewing opportunities year-round. In winter, the cooler temperatures can make hiking and exploring more comfortable, and the lack of crowds can offer a more peaceful experience. Some popular national parks to visit in winter include the Blue Mountains in New South Wales, the Grampians in Victoria, and the Flinders Ranges in South Australia.

## Chapter 2: Accommodations

Accommodations in Australia range from budget-friendly hostels to luxury resorts, with plenty of options in between. As a first-time visitor, it's important to consider your budget, location preferences, and the type of experience you want to have when choosing accommodations in Australia. Here are some of the most common types of accommodations you can expect to find:

### Hotels and Resorts

Hotels and resorts are a popular choice for travelers who want comfortable and convenient accommodations with all the necessary amenities. Australia has a wide range of hotels and resorts, from budget-friendly options to luxurious 5-star properties.

Budget-friendly hotels can range from around $50 to $100 AUD per night, while mid-range options can cost between $100 to $200 AUD per night. Luxury hotels and resorts can cost upwards of $300 AUD per night, with some of the most high-end properties charging $1,000 AUD or more per night.

Some of the most popular hotel and resort chains in Australia include Hilton, Sheraton, Marriott, Accor, and InterContinental. These chains have properties located in major cities and tourist destinations throughout the country, making them a convenient option for travelers who want a consistent level of quality and service.

## Hostels

Hostels are a popular choice for budget-conscious travelers, backpackers, and solo travelers who want to meet other travelers. Australia has a wide range of hostels, from basic dorm-style accommodations to more upscale properties with private rooms and en-suite bathrooms.

Hostels can be found in major cities, as well as in popular tourist destinations such as the Great Barrier Reef, the Whitsunday Islands, and the Gold Coast. Prices for hostel accommodations can vary widely, with dorm-style accommodations costing as little as $20 AUD per night and private rooms with en-suite bathrooms costing upwards of $100 AUD per night.

Some of the most popular hostel chains in Australia include YHA, Base Backpackers, Nomads, and Hostelworld. These chains have properties located throughout the country, making them a convenient option for budget travelers who want to explore multiple destinations.

## Bed and Breakfasts

Bed and breakfasts are a popular choice for travelers who want a more personalized and intimate experience. Bed and breakfasts are typically smaller properties with just a few rooms, and they often include breakfast in the room rate.

Bed and breakfasts can be found in both urban and rural areas of Australia, with many located in scenic locations such as wine regions, national parks, and coastal towns. Prices for bed and breakfast accommodations can vary widely, with some properties charging as little as $50 AUD per night and others costing upwards of $300 AUD per night.

**Airbnb and Vacation Rentals**

Airbnb and other vacation rental platforms have become increasingly popular in Australia in recent years, offering travelers the opportunity to stay in unique and often affordable accommodations. Vacation rentals can range from private rooms in someone's home to entire apartments, houses, or even villas.

Prices for vacation rentals can vary widely depending on the location, type of accommodation, and time of year. Some vacation rentals can be found for as little as $50 AUD per night, while others can cost several hundred dollars per night or more.

One of the advantages of vacation rentals is that they often come with a kitchen or kitchenette, allowing travelers to save money by preparing their own meals. Additionally, many vacation rentals are located in residential neighborhoods, offering a more authentic experience of local life.

**Camping and Caravan Parks**

Australia has a wealth of natural beauty, and camping and caravan parks are a popular choice for travelers who want to experience it firsthand. Camping and caravan parks can be found in national parks, coastal areas, and other scenic locations throughout the country.

Prices for camping and caravan park accommodations can vary widely depending on the location and level of amenities provided. Some basic campsites can be found for as little as $10 AUD per night, while more upscale camping and caravan parks can cost upwards of $50 AUD per night.

Many camping and caravan parks offer a range of amenities, including showers, toilets, laundry facilities, and cooking areas. Some parks also have cabins or caravan rentals available for those who prefer a bit more comfort.

**Luxury Lodges**

For those seeking the ultimate in luxury and exclusivity, Australia has a number of high-end lodges and resorts located in remote and scenic locations. These lodges often offer all-inclusive packages that include meals, activities, and guided tours.

Prices for luxury lodges can vary widely depending on the location and level of luxury offered. Some lodges can cost several thousand dollars per night, with prices typically including all meals, drinks, and activities.

Examples of luxury lodges in Australia include Longitude 131, located near Uluru in the Northern Territory, and Saffire Freycinet, located on Tasmania's east coast.

## Tips for Choosing Accommodations in Australia

When choosing accommodations in Australia, there are a few important factors to consider:

- Location: Australia is a large country, so it's important to choose accommodations that are located in the area you want to explore. If you're interested in exploring the Outback, for example, you'll want to choose accommodations located in or near the Outback region.
- Budget: Accommodation prices can vary widely in Australia, so it's important to have a budget in mind when choosing accommodations. Hostels and camping sites are typically the most budget-friendly options,

while luxury hotels and lodges can be quite expensive.
- Amenities: Consider the amenities that are important to you, such as a swimming pool, air conditioning, or free Wi-Fi. Many accommodations in Australia offer a range of amenities, so it's important to choose the ones that best fit your needs.
- Reviews: Before booking accommodations, be sure to read reviews from other travelers to get a sense of their experiences. Sites like TripAdvisor and Booking.com are great resources for finding reviews and ratings of accommodations in Australia.
- Season: As discussed earlier, the best time to visit Australia can vary depending on your interests and preferences. Be sure to consider the season when choosing accommodations, as some properties may be closed or have limited

availability during certain times of the year.

Overall, Australia offers a wide range of accommodations to suit all tastes and budgets. Whether you're looking for a budget-friendly hostel or a luxurious resort, you're sure to find the perfect place to stay during your visit to this incredible country.

## Recommendations for budget, mid-range, and luxury accommodations in different parts of the country

Australia is a country that offers a wide range of accommodation options for travelers with varying budgets and preferences. From budget-friendly hostels to luxury hotels, Australia has something to suit everyone's taste and budget. Here are some recommendations for budget, mid-range, and luxury accommodations in different parts of the country:

## Sydney

*Budget: Wake Up! Sydney Hostel*

Wake Up! Sydney Hostel is a budget-friendly option located in the heart of Sydney's central business district. The hostel offers both dormitory-style accommodations and private rooms, with prices starting at around $25 AUD per night for a bed in a dormitory room. The hostel also features a rooftop terrace, a communal kitchen, and a travel desk.

*Mid-Range: Vibe Hotel Sydney*

Vibe Hotel Sydney is a mid-range option located in the heart of Sydney's central business district. The hotel features stylishly designed rooms with modern amenities such as free Wi-Fi, flat-screen TVs, and mini fridges. Prices start at around $150 AUD per night.

*Luxury: The Langham, Sydney*

The Langham, Sydney is a luxury hotel located in the historic Rocks district of Sydney. The hotel features luxurious rooms and suites with views of the city or the harbor, as well as a range of amenities such as a spa, a fitness center, and an on-site restaurant. Prices start at around $400 AUD per night.

## Melbourne

*Budget: Space Hotel*

Space Hotel is a budget-friendly option located in the heart of Melbourne's central business district. The hostel offers both dormitory-style accommodations and private rooms, with prices starting at around $30 AUD per night for a bed in a dormitory room. The hostel also features a rooftop terrace, a communal kitchen, and a 24-hour reception desk.

*Mid-Range: The Victoria Hotel Melbourne*

The Victoria Hotel Melbourne is a mid-range option located in the heart of Melbourne's central business district. The hotel features modern rooms and suites with amenities such as flat-screen TVs, mini fridges, and free Wi-Fi. Prices start at around $100 AUD per night.

*Luxury: The Langham, Melbourne*

The Langham, Melbourne is a luxury hotel located in the heart of Melbourne's arts and entertainment district. The hotel features luxurious rooms and suites with views of the city or the Yarra River, as well as a range of amenities such as a spa, a fitness center, and an on-site restaurant. Prices start at around $300 AUD per night.

**Brisbane**

*Budget: Breeze Lodge*

Breeze Lodge is a budget-friendly option located in the vibrant Fortitude Valley neighborhood of Brisbane. The hostel offers both dormitory-style accommodations and private rooms, with prices starting at around $30 AUD per night for a bed in a dormitory room. The hostel also features a communal kitchen, a rooftop terrace, and a 24-hour reception desk.

*Mid-Range: The Johnson, Art Series Hotel*

The Johnson, Art Series Hotel is a mid-range option located in the trendy Spring Hill neighborhood of Brisbane. The hotel features stylishly designed rooms and suites with amenities such as flat-screen TVs, mini fridges, and free Wi-Fi. Prices start at around $150 AUD per night.

*Luxury: Emporium Hotel South Bank*

Emporium Hotel South Bank is a luxury hotel located in the vibrant South Bank neighborhood of Brisbane. The hotel features luxurious rooms and suites with views of the city or the river, as well as a range of amenities such as a spa, a fitness center, and an on-site restaurant. Prices start at around $300 AUD per night.

## Cairns

*Budget: Gilligan's Backpackers Hotel and Resort*

Gilligan's Backpackers Hotel and Resort is a budget-friendly option located in the heart of Cairns. The hostel offers both dormitory-style accommodations and private rooms, with prices starting at around $25 AUD per night for a bed in a dormitory room. The hostel also features a pool, a bar, and a communal kitchen.

*Mid-Range: Riley, a Crystalbrook Collection Resort*

Riley, a Crystalbrook Collection Resort is a mid-range option located in the vibrant Cairns Esplanade neighborhood. The hotel features modern rooms and suites with amenities such as flat-screen TVs, mini fridges, and free Wi-Fi. Prices start at around $200 AUD per night.

*Luxury: Pullman Reef Hotel Casino*

Pullman Reef Hotel Casino is a luxury hotel located in the heart of Cairns. The hotel features luxurious rooms and suites with views of the city or the ocean, as well as a range of amenities such as a spa, a fitness center, and an on-site casino. Prices start at around $400 AUD per night.

**Gold Coast**

*Budget: Surfers Paradise YHA*

Surfers Paradise YHA is a budget-friendly option located in the heart of Surfers Paradise, one of the Gold Coast's most popular neighborhoods. The hostel offers both dormitory-style accommodations and private rooms, with prices starting at around $30 AUD per night for a bed in a dormitory room. The hostel also features a pool, a bar, and a communal kitchen.

*Mid-Range: QT Gold Coast*

QT Gold Coast is a mid-range option located in the trendy Surfers Paradise neighborhood. The hotel features stylishly designed rooms and suites with amenities such as flat-screen TVs, mini fridges, and free Wi-Fi. Prices start at around $200 AUD per night.

*Luxury: Palazzo Versace*

Palazzo Versace is a luxury hotel located in the exclusive neighborhood of Main Beach on the Gold Coast. The hotel features luxurious rooms and suites with views of the ocean or the marina, as well as a range of amenities such as a spa, a fitness center, and an on-site restaurant. Prices start at around $500 AUD per night.

## Perth

*Budget: The Hive Hostel*

The Hive Hostel is a budget-friendly option located in the heart of Perth's central business district. The hostel offers both dormitory-style accommodations and private rooms, with prices starting at around $25 AUD per night for a bed in a dormitory room. The hostel also features a communal kitchen, a rooftop terrace, and a 24-hour reception desk.

*Mid-Range: DoubleTree by Hilton Perth Northbridge*

DoubleTree by Hilton Perth Northbridge is a mid-range option located in the vibrant Northbridge neighborhood of Perth. The hotel features modern rooms and suites with amenities such as flat-screen TVs, mini fridges, and free Wi-Fi. Prices start at around $150 AUD per night.

*Luxury: The Ritz-Carlton, Perth*

The Ritz-Carlton, Perth is a luxury hotel located on the banks of the Swan River in Perth. The hotel features luxurious rooms and suites with views of the river or the city, as well as a range of amenities such as a spa, a fitness center, and an on-site restaurant. Prices start at around $400 AUD per night.

Australia offers a wide range of accommodation options for travelers with varying budgets and preferences. From budget-friendly hostels to luxury hotels, there is something to suit everyone's taste and budget. When choosing an accommodation in Australia, it is important to consider the location, the amenities offered, and the price. With these recommendations, you can easily find the perfect accommodation for your next trip to Australia.

## Information on amenities and services offered by each type of accommodation

Accommodations in Australia offer a range of amenities and services to ensure that guests have a comfortable and enjoyable stay. Here is a breakdown of the amenities and services offered by each type of accommodation:

### Hotels

Hotels in Australia offer a range of amenities and services to cater to the needs of their guests. Some of the most common amenities and services offered by hotels include:

1. Room Service: Many hotels in Australia offer room service, allowing guests to order food and beverages to their room.
2. Wi-Fi: Most hotels in Australia offer free Wi-Fi to guests, allowing them to stay connected during their stay.

3. On-site Restaurant: Many hotels in Australia have an on-site restaurant, offering guests a convenient option for dining.
4. Fitness Center: Many hotels in Australia have a fitness center on-site, allowing guests to keep up with their workout routine while on vacation.
5. Swimming Pool: Many hotels in Australia have a swimming pool on-site, offering guests a refreshing way to cool off during their stay.
6. Concierge Service: Many hotels in Australia have a concierge service, allowing guests to get recommendations for local activities and attractions.
7. Business Center: Many hotels in Australia have a business center on-site, offering guests access to computers, printers, and other office equipment.

## Hostels

Hostels in Australia offer a range of amenities and services, often catering to the needs of budget-conscious travelers. Some of the most common amenities and services offered by hostels include:

1. Communal Kitchen: Many hostels in Australia have a communal kitchen, allowing guests to cook their own meals and save money on dining out.
2. Dormitory-Style Accommodations: Many hostels in Australia offer dormitory-style accommodations, allowing guests to save money on lodging.
3. Private Rooms: Many hostels in Australia offer private rooms, giving guests the option to have their own space.
4. Free Wi-Fi: Most hostels in Australia offer free Wi-Fi to guests.
5. Laundry Facilities: Many hostels in Australia have laundry facilities

on-site, allowing guests to do laundry during their stay.
6. Lockers: Many hostels in Australia have lockers available for guests to store their belongings.
7. Common Areas: Many hostels in Australia have common areas, such as a lounge or game room, where guests can socialize and meet other travelers.

**Guesthouses**

Guesthouses in Australia are often smaller and more intimate than hotels, offering a homey atmosphere for guests. Some of the most common amenities and services offered by guesthouses include:

1. Breakfast: Many guesthouses in Australia offer breakfast to guests.
2. Free Wi-Fi: Most guesthouses in Australia offer free Wi-Fi to guests.
3. Communal Areas: Many guesthouses in Australia have communal areas,

such as a lounge or garden, where guests can socialize.
4. Private Bathrooms: Many guesthouses in Australia offer private bathrooms for guests.
5. Laundry Facilities: Some guesthouses in Australia have laundry facilities on-site.
6. Personalized Service: Guesthouses in Australia often offer personalized service, with owners or staff able to give recommendations for local activities and attractions.

## Rental Properties

Rental properties in Australia are often fully furnished homes or apartments that are available for short-term stays. Some of the most common amenities and services offered by rental properties include:

1. Fully Equipped Kitchen: Rental properties in Australia often have fully

equipped kitchens, allowing guests to cook their own meals.
2. Free Wi-Fi: Most rental properties in Australia offer free Wi-Fi to guests.
3. Private Bathrooms: Rental properties in Australia often have private bathrooms for guests.
4. Laundry Facilities: Rental properties in Australia often have laundry facilities on-site.
5. Personalized Service: Some rental properties in Australia offer personalized

# Top Hotels in Australia

Australia has a wealth of luxurious and high-end hotels that cater to travelers looking for the ultimate in comfort and amenities.

Here are some of the top hotels in the country:

1. Emirates One&Only Wolgan Valley

The Emirates One&Only Wolgan Valley is a luxurious eco-resort located in the stunning

Blue Mountains. The resort features 40 individual villas, each with a private swimming pool, fireplace, and spacious veranda with views of the surrounding mountains. The resort also has a spa, fitness center, and gourmet restaurant, offering guests a truly luxurious and tranquil escape.

2. Park Hyatt Sydney

The Park Hyatt Sydney is one of the most iconic hotels in Australia, located on the waterfront with stunning views of the Sydney Opera House and Harbour Bridge. The hotel features luxurious guest rooms with floor-to-ceiling windows, a rooftop pool, and spa, and a world-class restaurant serving modern Australian cuisine.

3. Saffire Freycinet

The Saffire Freycinet is a luxurious retreat located on the east coast of Tasmania, offering stunning views of the Freycinet Peninsula and Wineglass Bay. The resort features 20 luxurious suites, each with a private balcony, fireplace, and outdoor bathtub. Guests can also enjoy a range of activities, including hiking, kayaking, and wildlife spotting, as well as gourmet dining and spa treatments.

4. Crown Towers Melbourne

The Crown Towers Melbourne is a luxurious hotel located in the heart of Melbourne's vibrant Southbank precinct. The hotel features luxurious guest rooms with views of the city or the Yarra River, a world-class spa, and fitness center, and a range of dining options, including a Japanese restaurant, a seafood grill, and a French bistro.

5. Longitude 131

Longitude 131 is a luxury eco-resort located in the heart of the Australian Outback, offering stunning views of Uluru (Ayers Rock) and the surrounding desert landscape. The resort features 15 luxurious tents, each with a private balcony and views of Uluru, as well as a world-class restaurant serving modern Australian cuisine and a range of activities, including guided walks, camel rides, and stargazing.

*Mid-Range Hotels*

For travelers looking for more affordable accommodations without sacrificing comfort and amenities, mid-range hotels are a great option. Here are some of the top mid-range hotels in Australia:

1. QT Sydney

The QT Sydney is a stylish and luxurious hotel located in the heart of Sydney's central business district. The hotel features spacious guest rooms with unique design features, a rooftop bar and lounge, and a range of dining options, including a modern Italian restaurant and a New York-style deli.

2. The Adnate Perth

The Adnate Perth is a vibrant and colorful hotel located in the heart of Perth's cultural district. The hotel features spacious guest rooms with murals by renowned Australian street artist Matt Adnate, a rooftop pool and bar, and a range of dining options, including a Mediterranean-inspired restaurant and a rooftop BBQ.

### 3. Ovolo The Valley Brisbane

Ovolo The Valley Brisbane is a stylish and modern hotel located in the trendy Fortitude Valley neighborhood of Brisbane. The hotel features spacious guest rooms with unique design features, a rooftop pool and bar, and a range of dining options, including a modern Asian restaurant and a speakeasy-style bar.

### 4. Sage Hotel Adelaide

Sage Hotel Adelaide is a stylish and modern hotel located in the heart of Adelaide's central business district. The hotel features spacious guest rooms with contemporary design features, a rooftop pool and bar, and a range of dining options, including a modern Australian restaurant and a casual cafe.

### 5. Shangri-La Hotel, Sydney

Located in the heart of Sydney, the Shangri-La Hotel offers luxurious accommodations with stunning views of the Sydney Opera House and Harbour Bridge. The hotel features several dining options, including the award-winning Altitude Restaurant, which offers panoramic views of the city skyline. The hotel also offers a spa, fitness center, and indoor pool.

Amenities:

- Panoramic views of the Sydney Opera House and Harbour Bridge
- Award-winning Altitude Restaurant
- Spa, fitness center, and indoor pool
- Business center and meeting rooms
- Free Wi-Fi
- 24-hour room service
- Concierge services

6. The Langham, Melbourne

The Langham in Melbourne is a luxurious hotel located on the banks of the Yarra River. The hotel features a spa, fitness center, indoor pool, and several dining options, including the award-winning Melba

Restaurant. The hotel also offers stunning views of the city skyline and is within walking distance of many popular attractions.

Amenities:

- Spa, fitness center, and indoor pool
- Award-winning Melba Restaurant
- Afternoon tea in the Aria Bar and Lounge
- Views of the city skyline and Yarra River
- Complimentary shuttle service within the city center
- Free Wi-Fi
- 24-hour room service
- Concierge services

7. Crown Towers, Perth

The Crown Towers in Perth offers luxurious accommodations with stunning views of the city skyline and the Swan River. The hotel features a spa, fitness center, indoor and outdoor pools, and several dining options, including the award-winning Epicurean Restaurant. The hotel is also connected to the Crown Perth complex, which includes a casino, theater, and several shopping and dining options.

Amenities:

- Spa, fitness center, and indoor and outdoor pools
- Award-winning Epicurean Restaurant
- Views of the city skyline and Swan River
- Direct access to the Crown Perth complex
- Free Wi-Fi
- 24-hour room service
- Concierge services

8. Four Seasons Hotel, Sydney

Located in the heart of Sydney, the Four Seasons Hotel offers luxurious accommodations with stunning views of the city skyline and Harbour Bridge. The hotel features several dining options, including the award-winning Kable's Restaurant. The hotel also offers a spa, fitness center, and outdoor pool.

Amenities:

- Views of the city skyline and Harbour Bridge
- Award-winning Kable's Restaurant
- Spa, fitness center, and outdoor pool
- Business center and meeting rooms
- Free Wi-Fi
- 24-hour room service
- Concierge services

## 9. COMO The Treasury, Perth

The COMO The Treasury in Perth is a luxurious hotel located in a restored 19th-century building. The hotel features a spa, fitness center, indoor pool, and several dining options, including the award-winning Wildflower Restaurant. The hotel also offers stunning views of the city skyline and is within walking distance of many popular attractions.

Amenities:

- Spa, fitness center, and indoor pool
- Award-winning Wildflower Restaurant
- Views of the city skyline
- Complimentary yoga and pilates classes
- Free Wi-Fi
- 24-hour room service
- Concierge services

Australia offers a diverse range of accommodations for visitors to choose from, including budget-friendly hostels, mid-range hotels, and luxurious resorts. Each type of accommodation offers unique amenities and services, making it important to consider individual preferences and budget when choosing a place to stay. From the bustling cities to the stunning natural landscapes, Australia has something to offer for every type of traveler.

## Chapter 3: Transportation

Transportation in Australia is modern and efficient, with a variety of options available for visitors to choose from. Whether you're exploring the city or traveling between destinations, there are numerous transportation options that can help you get around the country quickly and easily. In this section, we'll take a look at some of the most popular transportation options in Australia, including public transportation, taxis, rental cars, and more.

*Public Transportation*

Australia has an extensive network of public transportation options, including trains, buses, and trams, making it easy for visitors to get around the country. Public transportation is generally safe, reliable, and affordable, with a range of ticket options available depending on your needs.

*Trains*

Australia has an extensive rail network that connects most major cities and towns. The trains are modern, comfortable, and offer stunning views of the country's landscapes. Train travel in Australia can be a great way to see the country's scenic beauty, from the rugged outback to the lush green rainforests.

The national rail service is called the Great Southern Rail, and it offers a range of long-distance train journeys, including the famous Indian Pacific, which travels from

Sydney to Perth, and the Ghan, which travels from Darwin to Adelaide.

*Buses*

Buses are another popular form of public transportation in Australia, offering a convenient and affordable way to get around. Most major cities have their own bus network, and there are also long-distance bus services available for travel between cities.

One of the most popular bus companies in Australia is Greyhound, which offers a range of bus services across the country, including budget and luxury options. Another popular option is the Oz Experience, which provides hop-on, hop-off bus passes for backpackers and budget travelers.

*Trams*

Trams are a popular form of public transportation in some of Australia's major cities, including Melbourne and Adelaide.

The trams offer a convenient way to travel around the city center and provide a unique way to see the sights.

*Taxis*

Taxis are widely available in Australia and offer a convenient way to get around the city. Taxis are generally safe and reliable, but they can be more expensive than other forms of public transportation.

*Rental Cars*

Rental cars are a popular option for visitors who want to explore the country at their own pace. Rental cars are available from a range of companies, including major international brands and local companies. The cost of renting a car in Australia can vary depending on the type of car, the rental company, and the length of the rental.

Driving in Australia is generally safe and easy, with well-maintained roads and clear signage. However, visitors should be aware that Australia drives on the left-hand side of the road, which can take some getting used to for those who are not accustomed to it.

*Bicycles*

Bicycles are a popular form of transportation in some Australian cities, particularly in cities with a strong cycling culture like Melbourne and Sydney. Many cities have dedicated bike lanes, making it easy and safe to cycle around the city. There are also numerous bike rental companies available, making it easy for visitors to rent a bike for the day or longer.

*Air Travel*

Australia is a large country, and air travel is often the fastest and most convenient way to travel between destinations. Australia has numerous airports, including major international airports in cities like Sydney, Melbourne, and Brisbane, as well as smaller regional airports.

Australia's national carrier is Qantas, which offers a range of domestic and international flights. Other airlines that operate in Australia include Virgin Australia, Jetstar, and Tigerair.

Australia offers visitors a wide range of transportation options, making it easy to explore the country's diverse landscapes and attractions. Whether you prefer to travel by train, bus, car, or plane, there is a transportation option

## Options for getting around Australia, including public transportation, taxis, rental cars, and tours

Australia is a vast country, and getting around can be a challenge for visitors. Fortunately, there are a variety of transportation options available to suit every budget and travel style. From public transportation to rental cars, taxis to tours, there are many ways to explore Australia's unique landscape and attractions. In this section, we will cover the different options for getting around Australia.

*Public Transportation*

Australia has an extensive public transportation network, with trains, buses, and trams connecting cities and towns across the country. The major cities all have their own public transportation systems, which are generally reliable and affordable.

*Trains*

Australia's train system is operated by several different companies, including Great Southern Rail, NSW TrainLink, and Queensland Rail. These trains connect major cities and towns across the country, offering a comfortable and scenic way to travel.

One of the most famous train journeys in Australia is the Indian Pacific, which travels from Sydney to Perth via Adelaide. The journey takes three days and covers over

4,000 kilometers, passing through the stunning Outback and offering passengers breathtaking views of the Australian landscape.

Another popular train journey is the Ghan, which travels from Adelaide to Darwin via Alice Springs. This journey also takes three days and covers over 2,900 kilometers, passing through the heart of Australia's Red Centre.

*Trams*

Melbourne is the only city in Australia with an extensive tram network, which covers the central business district and surrounding suburbs. Trams in Melbourne are a popular way to get around the city, with frequent services and affordable fares.

*Buses*

Buses are a common mode of transportation in Australia, particularly in regional areas where train services are limited. The major cities all have their own bus networks, with frequent services and affordable fares.

In addition to public transportation, there are also several private companies that offer bus tours and day trips to popular attractions across the country.

*Taxis*

Taxis are readily available in all major cities and towns in Australia. Taxis are metered, with fares based on distance traveled and time spent in the vehicle. Tipping is not expected, but rounding up to the nearest dollar is common.

Ride-sharing services such as Uber and Ola are also available in many parts of Australia, providing a convenient and affordable alternative to traditional taxis.

*Rental Cars*

Renting a car is a popular way to explore Australia's vast and varied landscape. There are several international car rental companies operating in Australia, as well as local companies.

Renting a car gives you the freedom to travel at your own pace and explore areas that are off the beaten track. However, it's important to note that Australia has strict driving laws, and it's important to familiarize yourself with these laws before hitting the road.

*Tours*

If you prefer not to drive, or if you're looking for a more organized way to explore Australia, there are many tour companies offering a wide range of tours and excursions.

From day trips to multi-day tours, there are tours available to suit every interest and budget. Some of the most popular types of tours include:

- Wildlife tours: Australia is home to a wide variety of unique wildlife, and there are many tour companies offering opportunities to see animals such as kangaroos, koalas, and crocodiles in their natural habitat.
- Wine tours: Australia is also known for its world-class wines, and there are many tours available that visit some of the country's top wineries and vineyards.
- Adventure tours: For those seeking an adrenaline rush, there are many adventure tours available, including hiking, kayaking, and surfing.
- Cultural tours: Australia has a rich Aboriginal history, and there are many

tours available that explore this heritage and offer opportunities to learn about the country's indigenous cultures.
- City tours: Finally, if you're short on time or prefer a more guided experience, city tours can be a great option. Many cities in Australia offer guided tours of their main attractions, either on foot, by bus, or even by bike. These tours can provide a great overview of the city's history and culture, and are often led by knowledgeable and enthusiastic guides.

Some popular city tours in Australia include the Big Bus tours in Sydney and Melbourne, the free walking tours in Brisbane and Adelaide, and the bike tours in Perth and Hobart.

City tours can vary in length, price, and itinerary, so it is important to research and choose the one that best fits your interests and budget. They can be a great way to see the main attractions in a short amount of time and to learn about the city's history and culture from a local perspective.

Australia offers a variety of options for transportation, including public transportation, taxis, rental cars, and tours. Each mode of transportation has its own advantages and disadvantages, and the best option will depend on your travel style and budget. It is important to research and plan ahead to ensure a smooth and enjoyable travel experience.

## Chapter 4: Food and Drink

Australia is a country with a diverse and rich food culture that reflects its unique history, geography, and people. From traditional Aboriginal cuisine to modern fusion dishes, Australia has something to offer every foodie. In this guide, we will explore the food and drink scene in Australia, including popular dishes, local specialties, and tips for dining out.

## Popular Dishes

Australian cuisine is influenced by the many cultures that have settled in the country over the years, including British, Asian, Mediterranean, and Aboriginal. Some popular dishes that you can find all over Australia include:

- Meat pies: A savory pastry filled with beef, chicken, or lamb, often served with tomato sauce.
- Fish and chips: A British classic, battered and fried fish served with thick-cut fries.
- Barbecue: Australians love to grill, and barbecued meat and seafood are a staple at many gatherings.
- Vegemite: A salty spread made from yeast extract, often enjoyed on toast for breakfast.
- Lamingtons: A sponge cake covered in chocolate icing and coconut, often served at morning or afternoon tea.

- Pavlova: A dessert made from a meringue base topped with whipped cream and fresh fruit.
- Tim Tams: A chocolate-covered biscuit with a creamy filling, often enjoyed with a cup of tea or coffee.

**Local Specialties**

In addition to these popular dishes, each region in Australia has its own unique specialties and local flavors. Here are some examples:

- Seafood: With over 36,000 kilometers of coastline, Australia has an abundance of fresh seafood, including oysters, prawns, and crayfish. The Sydney rock oyster and Moreton Bay bug are two popular local specialties.
- Kangaroo and emu: As native animals, kangaroo and emu meat are considered traditional Australian fare. These meats are low in fat and high in

protein, and can be found on the menu at many restaurants.
- Barramundi: A type of fish found in northern Australia, barramundi is often grilled or pan-fried and served with a side of salad or vegetables.
- Tasmanian whisky: Tasmania is known for its high-quality whisky, with several distilleries producing award-winning spirits.
- Wine: Australia is home to some of the world's best wine regions, including the Barossa Valley, Margaret River, and Hunter Valley. Shiraz and chardonnay are two popular Australian varietals.

**Dining Out**

Australia has a vibrant dining scene, with a wide range of restaurants, cafes, and bars offering everything from casual eats to fine dining experiences. Here are some tips for dining out in Australia:

- Tipping: While tipping is not expected in Australia, it is appreciated for exceptional service. A tip of 10% is considered generous.
- Reservations: Many popular restaurants in Australia require reservations, especially on weekends or during peak season. It is recommended to book in advance to avoid disappointment.
- BYO: Many restaurants in Australia allow customers to bring their own wine (BYO), for a small corkage fee.
- Dietary restrictions: Many restaurants in Australia offer vegetarian, vegan, and gluten-free options on their menu. If you have a specific dietary restriction, it is best to inquire before making a reservation.
- Breakfast and brunch: Australians love their breakfast and brunch, and there are many cafes and restaurants that specialize in these meals. Avocado

toast and flat whites are two popular breakfast items.

## Drinks

In addition to its food scene, Australia also has a vibrant drinking culture. Here are some popular drinks to try:

*Beer:*

Beer is one of the most popular alcoholic beverages in Australia, and there are many local breweries producing craft beers. Some popular beer brands include Victoria Bitter, Tooheys, and Carlton Draught. Australia is also home to some great microbreweries, producing unique and flavorful beers that are worth trying.

*Wine:*

Australia is also famous for its wine industry, with many world-renowned wine regions producing a variety of wines. Some of the most popular wine regions include the

Barossa Valley, Margaret River, Hunter Valley, and Yarra Valley. Shiraz, Cabernet Sauvignon, Chardonnay, and Pinot Noir are some of the most common grape varieties grown in Australia.

*Cocktails:*

Australian bartenders are known for their creativity and innovation when it comes to cocktails. Some popular cocktails in Australia include the classic Martini, Cosmopolitan, Margarita, and Mojito. Australian bartenders also like to experiment with local ingredients such as eucalyptus, lemon myrtle, and native berries to create unique and flavorful cocktails.

*Spirits:*

Australia has a thriving spirits industry, with many local distilleries producing high-quality spirits. Some popular Australian spirits include Bundaberg Rum, Archie Rose Gin, and Limeburners Whiskey. Australian distillers often use locally sourced ingredients such as native botanicals, fruits, and herbs to give their spirits a unique flavor profile.

**Non-Alcoholic Drinks:**

For those who prefer non-alcoholic drinks, Australia has plenty of options as well. Some popular non-alcoholic beverages include fresh juices, smoothies, and mocktails. Australia is also famous for its coffee culture, with many specialty coffee shops serving high-quality coffee using locally roasted beans. Tea is also a popular beverage in Australia, with a wide range of herbal teas and tea blends available.

Australia has a vibrant drinking culture with a wide range of alcoholic and non-alcoholic beverages to choose from. Whether you prefer beer, wine, cocktails, or spirits, there is something for everyone to enjoy.

## Overview of Australian cuisine and dining options, including recommended restaurants and local specialties

Australia is a country known for its vast landscapes, beautiful beaches, and unique wildlife. However, the country's cuisine and dining options are also worth exploring. With influences from indigenous Australian cuisine, British, Asian, and Mediterranean cuisine, Australia offers a diverse range of dishes and flavors that reflect its multiculturalism. In this guide, we will take a closer look at Australia's cuisine and dining options, including recommended restaurants and local specialties.

## Overview of Australian Cuisine

Australian cuisine is a blend of indigenous Australian, British, and European influences, along with flavors from Asia, the Middle East, and the Americas. Indigenous Australian cuisine is based on the traditional foods and cooking methods of the Aboriginal and Torres Strait Islander peoples. These foods include bush tucker such as kangaroo, emu, crocodile, and various types of seafood, along with native plants like wattleseed, lemon myrtle, and macadamia nuts. Indigenous Australians also used a range of cooking techniques, including grilling, smoking, and baking in earth ovens.

The British influence on Australian cuisine can be traced back to the colonial period when British settlers arrived in the country. They introduced foods like roast beef, pies, and fish and chips. Later, European migrants brought their own culinary traditions, such as Italian pasta, French pastries, and Greek meze.

Asian cuisine has also had a significant impact on Australian cuisine, with Chinese, Vietnamese, and Thai dishes being popular choices. Middle Eastern cuisine has also gained popularity in recent years, with dishes like falafel and hummus becoming common.

In terms of dining options, Australia has a wide range of choices, from casual eateries to high-end restaurants. Many of these establishments use locally sourced ingredients to create dishes that reflect the flavors of the region.

## Recommended Restaurants

Australia has many outstanding restaurants that offer a variety of cuisines and dining experiences. Here are some recommended restaurants in various cities:

1. Attica, Melbourne - Attica is a fine-dining restaurant that has received international acclaim for its innovative use of local ingredients. Chef Ben Shewry's tasting menu includes dishes like "Potato cooked in the earth it was grown," which features potato cooked in a fire pit and served with a smoked eel dip.
2. Quay, Sydney - Quay is a waterfront restaurant that offers stunning views of Sydney Harbour. Chef Peter Gilmore's menu features dishes like "Mud crab congee," which is a modern take on the classic Chinese comfort food.
3. Ester, Sydney - Ester is a casual eatery that specializes in wood-fired cooking.

The menu features dishes like grilled octopus with nduja and finger lime, and wood-fired flatbread with anchovy butter.
4. The Agrarian Kitchen Eatery, Hobart - The Agrarian Kitchen Eatery is located in Tasmania and serves dishes made with locally sourced ingredients. The menu changes frequently but may include dishes like wood-grilled lamb with fermented garlic and rosemary.
5. Orana, Adelaide - Orana is a fine-dining restaurant that celebrates indigenous Australian cuisine. Chef Jock Zonfrillo's tasting menu includes dishes like kangaroo with native pepperberry and muntries.

**Local Specialties**

Australia has many local specialties that visitors should try during their stay. Here are some examples:

1. Vegemite - Vegemite is a popular spread made from yeast extract. Australians often spread it on toast or sandwiches for breakfast.
2. Meat pies - Meat pies are a classic Australian snack that consists of a pastry shell filled with meat and gravy. They are often served with tomato sauce (ketchup) and are a popular food at sporting events.
3. Tim Tams - Tim Tams are a popular biscuit (cookie) in Australia. They consist of two chocolate biscuits filled with chocolate cream and coated in a layer of chocolate. Tim Tams have become so popular that there are now many different flavors available, including caramel, dark chocolate, and white chocolate.
4. Pavlova - Pavlova is a dessert that is claimed by both Australia and New Zealand. It is a meringue cake that is topped with whipped cream and fresh

fruit, such as kiwi fruit, strawberries, and passionfruit.
5. Barramundi - Barramundi is a popular fish that is native to Australia's Northern Territory. It is a firm, white-fleshed fish that is often grilled or pan-fried and served with lemon and herbs.
6. Lamingtons - Lamingtons are a traditional Australian dessert that consists of sponge cake dipped in chocolate and coated in desiccated coconut. They are often served at afternoon tea or as a treat for children's birthday parties.
7. Chiko Roll - The Chiko Roll is a snack food that was invented in Australia in the 1950s. It consists of a savory filling of meat and vegetables that is wrapped in pastry and deep-fried. It is often served with tomato sauce (ketchup) and is a popular choice at fast-food outlets.

## Dining Options

Australia offers a range of dining options to suit all budgets and tastes. Here are some examples:

1. Cafes - Australia has a thriving cafe culture, with many cafes serving breakfast and lunch. Popular dishes include smashed avocado on toast, eggs Benedict, and acai bowls.

2. Food markets - Many cities in Australia have food markets that offer a range of street food and artisanal products.

Examples include the Queen Victoria Market in Melbourne and the Adelaide Central Market.

3. Food trucks - Food trucks are becoming increasingly popular in Australia, offering a range of street food from around the world. Some popular options include burgers, tacos, and gourmet hot dogs.
4. Pubs - Pubs are a popular choice for casual dining in Australia, with many offering hearty pub grub such as chicken parma (chicken schnitzel topped with tomato sauce and melted cheese) and bangers and mash (sausages and mashed potato).
5. Fine dining restaurants - Australia has many high-end restaurants that offer tasting menus and degustation menus. These restaurants often focus on locally sourced ingredients and innovative cooking techniques.

Australia's cuisine and dining options reflect the country's multiculturalism and diverse landscape. With influences from indigenous Australian cuisine, British, European, Asian, and Middle Eastern cuisine, Australia offers a wide range of dishes and flavors that are worth exploring. Whether you're looking for fine dining, casual eateries, or street food, Australia has something to offer everyone. So next time you visit Australia, be sure to try some of the local specialties and explore the country's vibrant dining scene.

**Tips on finding the best food and drink experiences, such as local markets, food tours, and cooking classes**

If you're planning a trip to Australia, one of the best ways to explore the country's diverse cuisine is by seeking out local markets, food tours, and cooking classes. Here are some tips on finding the best food and drink experiences in Australia.

1. Research the Local Cuisine

Before you arrive in Australia, take the time to research the local cuisine. Australia's food culture is heavily influenced by its indigenous population, as well as European, Asian, and Middle Eastern immigration. Each region of Australia has its own distinct culinary traditions and specialties.

For example, if you're traveling to Melbourne, you'll want to try the city's famous coffee culture and brunch scene. If you're visiting the Northern Territory, you might want to try barramundi, a popular local fish. Researching local food blogs, restaurant reviews, and travel guides can give you an idea of what dishes and flavors to look out for.

2. Explore Local Markets

Australia has a vibrant food market scene, with markets in almost every major city. Visiting local markets is a great way to sample fresh, locally sourced produce and support small businesses.

One of the most popular markets in Australia is the Queen Victoria Market in Melbourne. This historic market has been operating for over 140 years and offers a wide range of food stalls, fresh produce, and artisanal products. Other notable markets include the Adelaide Central Market, the Sydney Fish Market, and the Salamanca Market in Hobart.

3. Take a Food Tour

Food tours are a great way to explore a new destination's cuisine and learn about its history and culture. Australia has many food tour operators that offer a range of experiences, from street food tours to fine dining experiences.

In Melbourne, you can take a walking food tour of the city's laneways and hidden bars, or a coffee tour of the city's famous cafe scene. In Sydney, you can take a tour of the city's vibrant Chinatown, or a seafood tour of the city's fish markets. Food tours are also available in other cities, including Brisbane, Adelaide, and Perth.

4. Sign Up for a Cooking Class

Taking a cooking class is a great way to learn about a new cuisine and develop new skills in the kitchen. Australia has many cooking schools and classes that offer a range of experiences, from beginner classes to masterclasses with celebrity chefs.

In Melbourne, you can take a cooking class at the famous Queen Victoria Market, where you'll learn to cook with local produce and ingredients. In Sydney, you can take a cooking class at the Sydney Seafood School, where you'll learn to cook with fresh seafood. Other notable cooking schools include the Adelaide Central Market Cooking School and the Spirit House in Queensland.

5. Look for Local Specialty Restaurants

Australia is home to many unique and innovative restaurants that specialize in local cuisine and ingredients. These restaurants offer a great way to sample the country's culinary traditions and experience new flavors.

In Melbourne, you can visit Attica, a restaurant that is known for its use of native Australian ingredients and its innovative tasting menu. In Sydney, you can visit Quay, a restaurant that is famous for its fine dining experience and views of the Sydney Opera House. Other notable restaurants include Brae in Victoria, Tetsuya's in Sydney, and Orana in Adelaide.

6. Ask the Locals

One of the best ways to find the best food and drink experiences in Australia is to ask the locals. Australians are proud of their cuisine and are often happy to share their favorite restaurants, markets, and food tours.

If you're staying in a hotel or hostel, ask the staff for recommendations. If you're eating at a restaurant, ask the server for their favorite local dishes. Strike up a conversation with locals at a market or on a food tour and ask for their recommendations.

7. Use Food Apps

There are many food apps available that can help you find the best food and drink experiences in Australia. Apps like Yelp, Zomato, and TripAdvisor can provide reviews, ratings, and recommendations for restaurants and food tours in your area.

You can also use food delivery apps like Uber Eats and Deliveroo to sample local cuisine from the comfort of your accommodation. These apps often feature local restaurants that may not be as well-known to tourists.

8. Attend Food Festivals

Australia is home to many food festivals throughout the year, which offer a great way to sample local cuisine and meet other food enthusiasts. Some of the most popular festivals include the Melbourne Food and Wine Festival, the Sydney Good Food Month, and the Taste of Tasmania.

These festivals often feature food stalls, cooking demonstrations, wine tastings, and live entertainment. They can be a great way to experience local culture and cuisine in a festive atmosphere.

### 9. Try Street Food

Australia has a vibrant street food scene, with food trucks and pop-up stalls offering a range of international and local cuisine. Trying street food is a great way to sample local flavors and support small businesses.

In Melbourne, you can visit the Food Truck Park, which features a rotating selection of food trucks serving everything from tacos to burgers. In Sydney, you can visit the Night

Noodle Markets, a popular annual event that features Asian street food vendors. Other notable street food scenes include Brisbane's Eat Street Northshore and Perth's Twilight Hawkers Market.

10. Explore Wine Regions

Australia is famous for its wine regions, which produce some of the world's best-known wines. Visiting a wine region is a great way to sample local wines and learn about the country's wine-making traditions.

Some of the most popular wine regions in Australia include the Barossa Valley in South Australia, the Margaret River region in Western Australia, and the Hunter Valley in New South Wales. Many wine regions offer wine tastings, vineyard tours, and fine dining experiences.

Australia offers a wide range of food and drink experiences, from local markets to cooking classes and wine regions. By doing your research, exploring local markets and food tours, trying street food, and asking locals for recommendations, you can sample the best of Australia's diverse cuisine.

## Chapter 5: Activities and Attractions

Australia is a vast and diverse country that offers a wealth of activities and attractions for visitors to explore. From natural wonders to cultural landmarks, there is something for everyone to enjoy. In this guide, we will explore some of the top activities and attractions in Australia.

1. Visit the Great Barrier Reef

The Great Barrier Reef is one of the world's most impressive natural wonders, and it is the largest coral reef system in the world.

Located off the coast of Queensland, the Great Barrier Reef is home to a diverse array of marine life, including fish, turtles, sharks, and dolphins.

Visitors can explore the reef through a variety of activities, including snorkeling, scuba diving, and glass-bottom boat tours. The reef is also a popular destination for sailing, fishing, and other water sports.

2. Take a Road Trip

Australia is a great destination for road trips, as it offers vast and varied landscapes to explore. One of the most popular road trips is the Great Ocean Road, which stretches for over 240 kilometers along the southern coast of Victoria.

The road winds through beautiful coastal scenery, including the Twelve Apostles, a series of limestone stacks that rise out of the ocean. Other popular road trips include the Nullarbor Plain in Western Australia and the Red Centre Way in the Northern Territory.

3. Explore the Outback

The Australian Outback is a vast and rugged region that covers much of the country's interior. It is home to unique wildlife, stunning natural landmarks, and rich Indigenous culture.

Visitors can explore the Outback through a variety of activities, including hiking, camping, and guided tours. Some of the most popular destinations include Uluru (also known as Ayers Rock), the Kata Tjuta (also known as the Olgas), and Kakadu National Park.

4. Visit Sydney

Sydney is one of Australia's most iconic cities, known for its stunning harbor, vibrant nightlife, and iconic landmarks. Visitors can explore the city's many attractions, including the Sydney Opera

House, the Harbour Bridge, and Bondi Beach.

Sydney is also home to many museums, galleries, and cultural institutions, including the Australian Museum and the Art Gallery of New South Wales. Visitors can also sample the city's diverse food and drink scene, which includes everything from fine dining restaurants to trendy cafes and bars.

5. Discover Indigenous Culture

Australia is home to a rich and diverse Indigenous culture, with over 500 different Indigenous groups throughout the country. Visitors can learn about Indigenous culture through a variety of experiences, including guided tours, art exhibits, and cultural events.

Some of the most popular destinations for Indigenous culture include Uluru and the Red Centre, where visitors can learn about the Anangu people, who have lived in the region for over 60,000 years. Other popular destinations include the Northern Territory, Western Australia, and Queensland.

6. Experience Wildlife

Australia is home to a unique and diverse array of wildlife, including kangaroos, koalas, and wombats. Visitors can experience Australian wildlife through a variety of activities, including wildlife tours, national parks, and zoos.

Some of the most popular destinations for wildlife include the Kangaroo Island in South Australia, where visitors can see kangaroos, wallabies, and other native animals in their natural habitat. Other popular destinations include the Lone Pine Koala Sanctuary in Brisbane and the Taronga Zoo in Sydney.

7. Explore National Parks

Australia is home to over 500 national parks, which offer a range of natural beauty and outdoor activities. Visitors can explore national parks through hiking, camping, and guided tours.

Some of the most popular national parks include the Blue Mountains National Park in New South Wales, which features stunning mountain scenery and waterfalls, and the Daintree National Park in Queensland, which is home to a variety of unique flora and fauna, including the endangered cassowary bird.

Other popular national parks include the Great Otway National Park in Victoria, which offers beautiful coastal scenery and ancient rainforests, and the Cradle Mountain-Lake St. Clair National Park in Tasmania, which features dramatic mountain landscapes and crystal-clear lakes.

8. Visit Wine Regions

Australia is known for its world-class wine regions, including the Barossa Valley in South Australia, the Hunter Valley in New South Wales, and the Margaret River region in Western Australia. Visitors can explore these regions through wine tours, which offer tastings and behind-the-scenes experiences at wineries.

Some tours also include visits to local food producers and restaurants, allowing visitors to sample the best of the region's culinary offerings. In addition to wine tours, many wine regions also offer bike tours, hot air balloon rides, and other outdoor activities.

9. Experience Festivals and Events

Australia is home to a variety of festivals and events throughout the year, from cultural celebrations to music festivals. Some of the most popular events include the Sydney Mardi Gras, a colorful LGBTQ+ parade and festival held every February, and the Melbourne Cup, one of Australia's biggest horse racing events held every November.

Other popular events include the Vivid Sydney Festival, a light and music festival held in May and June, and the Adelaide Fringe Festival, an annual arts festival held in February and March. Visitors can also find smaller festivals and events throughout the country, celebrating everything from food and wine to sports and culture.

10. Enjoy Beaches

Australia is home to some of the world's most beautiful beaches, with over 10,000 beaches stretching along its coastline. Visitors can enjoy everything from secluded coves to popular surf beaches, and everything in between.

Some of the most popular beaches include Bondi Beach in Sydney, which is known for its trendy cafes and surf culture, and Surfers Paradise in Queensland, which is known for its high-rise hotels and nightlife. Other popular beaches include Whitehaven Beach in the Whitsunday Islands, which is known for its pristine white sand, and Cable Beach in Broome, which is known for its stunning sunsets and camel rides.

Australia offers a wide variety of activities and attractions for visitors to explore, from natural wonders to cultural landmarks. Whether you're interested in wildlife, wine, or beaches, there is something for everyone to enjoy in Australia. By planning your trip ahead of time and researching the best experiences, you can make the most of your time in this incredible country.

## Overview of the top things to do and see in Australia, including museums, landmarks, outdoor activities, and cultural experiences

Australia is a vast and diverse country with a wide range of attractions and activities for visitors to enjoy. From stunning natural wonders to iconic landmarks and cultural experiences, there is no shortage of things to see and do in this incredible country. In this guide, we will provide an overview of the top things to do and see in Australia, including museums, landmarks, outdoor activities, and cultural experiences.

1. Visit Uluru (Ayers Rock)

One of the most iconic landmarks in Australia is Uluru, also known as Ayers Rock. Located in the heart of the Australian Outback, Uluru is a massive sandstone rock formation that rises 348 meters above the desert floor. It is sacred to the Anangu people, who have lived in the area for tens of thousands of years.

Visitors can explore the area around Uluru on foot or by bike, and there are a variety of tours and experiences available, including sunrise and sunset tours, helicopter tours, and cultural tours led by Anangu guides. The nearby Kata Tjuta (The Olgas) rock formation is also worth a visit, with its towering red rocks and stunning scenery.

2. Explore the Great Barrier Reef

The Great Barrier Reef is one of the world's most famous natural wonders, stretching for over 2,300 kilometers along the coast of Queensland. It is home to a diverse range of marine life, including colorful coral, tropical fish, turtles, and whales.

Visitors can explore the Great Barrier Reef through snorkeling and diving tours, glass-bottom boat tours, and helicopter tours. There are also a number of island resorts located within the reef, offering visitors the opportunity to relax and soak up the stunning natural beauty of this incredible destination.

3. Visit Sydney Opera House

One of the most recognizable landmarks in Australia is the Sydney Opera House, located in Sydney Harbour. Designed by Danish architect Jorn Utzon, the Opera House is a masterpiece of modern architecture, featuring a series of sail-like shells that are covered in white tiles.

Visitors can take a guided tour of the Opera House, which provides a behind-the-scenes look at the iconic venue, including its theaters, rehearsal spaces, and production facilities. There are also a variety of shows and performances held at the Opera House throughout the year, including opera, ballet, and theater.

4. Explore the Australian Museum

The Australian Museum, located in Sydney, is the country's oldest museum, and features an extensive collection of natural history and cultural artifacts. Visitors can explore the museum's exhibits on everything from dinosaurs and fossils to Australian wildlife and indigenous culture.

Highlights of the museum include the Dinosaur Gallery, which features skeletons and fossils of prehistoric creatures, and the Indigenous Australians exhibition, which explores the rich cultural heritage of Australia's indigenous peoples.

5. Go on a Wildlife Safari

Australia is home to a wide range of unique and fascinating wildlife, including kangaroos, koalas, wallabies, and wombats. Visitors can go on wildlife safaris throughout the country, either on foot or by 4WD vehicle, and can even take part in nocturnal tours to see animals in their natural habitats at night.

Some of the best places to see wildlife in Australia include the Kangaroo Island Wildlife Park in South Australia, which features a range of Australian animals, including kangaroos, koalas, and echidnas, and the Taronga Western Plains Zoo in New South Wales, which features over 4,000 animals from around the world.

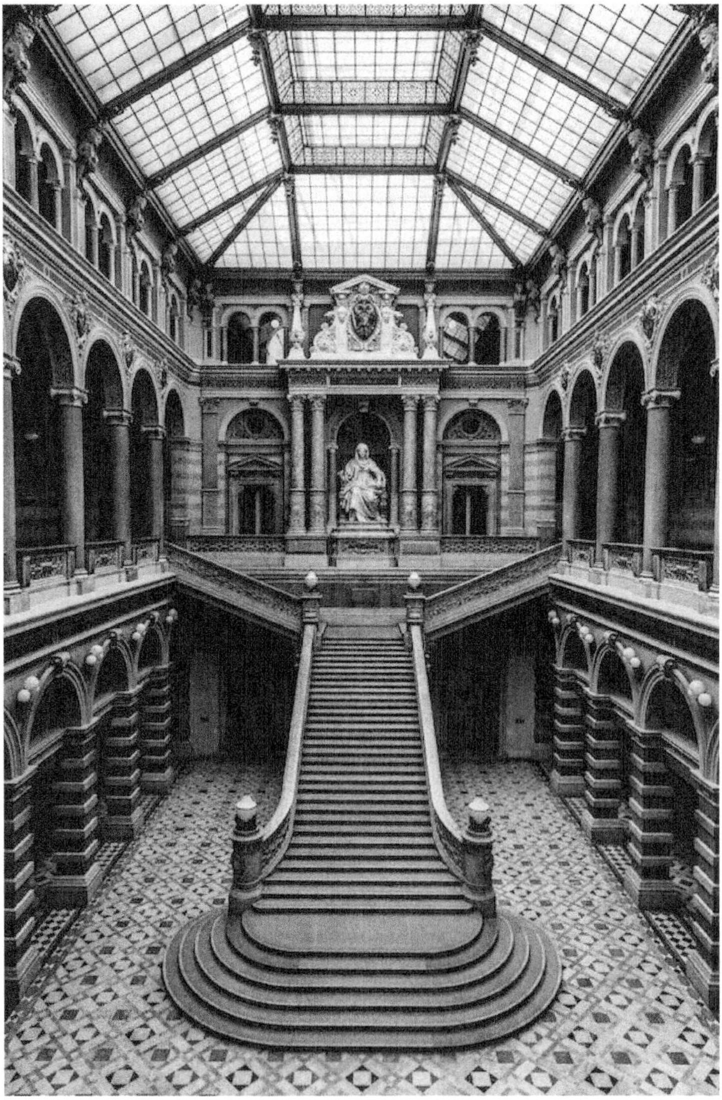

## 6. Visit the National Gallery of Australia

The National Gallery of Australia, located in Canberra, is the country's largest art museum, featuring over 160,000 works of art, including paintings, sculptures, and photographs. The museum's collection includes works by both Australian and international artists, with a particular focus on contemporary art.

Visitors can explore the museum's exhibitions on their own, or take a guided tour to learn more about the works on display. Some of the highlights of the museum's collection include Sidney Nolan's "Ned Kelly" series, a collection of paintings that depict the legendary outlaw, and Jackson Pollock's "Blue Poles," a large-scale abstract painting that is considered one of the most important works of art in the country.

## 7. Explore the Great Ocean Road

The Great Ocean Road is one of the most scenic drives in Australia, stretching for over 240 kilometers along the coast of Victoria. The road passes by stunning natural landmarks such as the Twelve Apostles, a series of limestone stacks that rise out of the sea, and the Great Otway National Park, which features rugged coastline and lush rainforest.

Visitors can explore the Great Ocean Road on a guided tour, or drive the route themselves, stopping at scenic lookouts and historic towns along the way. The region is also known for its excellent surfing beaches, and visitors can take surf lessons or rent a board to ride the waves themselves.

## 8. Visit the Royal Botanic Garden in Melbourne

The Royal Botanic Garden in Melbourne is one of the city's most popular attractions, featuring over 8,500 plant species from around the world. The garden covers over

38 hectares, and includes a variety of themed gardens, such as the Rose Garden, the Tropical Hothouse, and the Herb Garden.

Visitors can explore the gardens on their own, or take a guided tour to learn more about the plants and their histories. The garden also hosts a variety of events and exhibitions throughout the year, including outdoor concerts and art installations.

9. Experience Aboriginal Culture

Australia's indigenous peoples have a rich and diverse cultural heritage, and visitors can learn about their history and traditions through a variety of experiences and activities. One popular option is to take part in a cultural tour led by an indigenous guide, which can include activities such as bushwalks, storytelling, and traditional dance performances.

Visitors can also visit indigenous cultural centers and museums throughout the country, such as the Tjapukai Aboriginal Cultural Park in Queensland, which features interactive exhibits and performances that showcase indigenous culture, and the Museum of Contemporary Aboriginal Art in Sydney, which features works by contemporary indigenous artists.

10. Go on a Wine Tour in the Barossa Valley

The Barossa Valley, located in South Australia, is one of the country's premier wine regions, known for its rich history and excellent wine. Visitors can go on wine tours throughout the region, exploring its many wineries and tasting rooms, and learning about the history and production of the wines.

Some of the top wineries to visit in the Barossa Valley include Seppeltsfield, which features a range of wines and an historic estate, and Henschke, which is known for its high-quality Shiraz and Riesling wines.

Visitors can also sample local cheeses and gourmet foods as part of their wine tour experience.

Australia is a country full of incredible sights, experiences, and activities, and visitors have no shortage of options to choose from when planning their trip. From natural wonders to cultural landmarks, wildlife safaris to wine tours, there is something for everyone in this amazing country. No matter what your interests or preferences, a trip to Australia is sure to be an unforgettable experience.

## **Tips on finding the best activities and attractions, such as guided tours and off-the-beaten-path experiences**

When it comes to planning a trip to a new destination, finding the best activities and attractions can be a daunting task. While popular tourist destinations and landmarks are a great place to start, it's often the off-the-beaten-path experiences that truly make a trip memorable. Here are some tips for finding the best activities and attractions, including guided tours and off-the-beaten-path experiences, during your travels in Australia.

1. Research and plan ahead

One of the best ways to ensure you have a great experience during your travels is to research and plan ahead. Use travel guides, online forums, and recommendations from friends and family to create a list of potential activities and attractions to visit. Be sure to read reviews from other travelers, and pay attention to any warnings or safety concerns.

By planning ahead, you'll also have a better idea of what to expect in terms of pricing, time requirements, and logistics. This can help you avoid wasting time and money on activities that aren't worth it, and ensure that you make the most of your time in Australia.

2. Look for guided tours

Guided tours are a great way to explore a new destination and learn about its history, culture, and landmarks. They can also be a great way to meet other travelers and make new friends.

There are many different types of guided tours available in Australia, including walking tours, bike tours, food tours, and wildlife tours. Some tours are led by locals, while others are led by experienced tour guides. Be sure to research different tour companies and read reviews to find the best fit for your interests and budget.

3. Consider off-the-beaten-path experiences

While popular tourist attractions are a must-see, some of the best experiences can be found off the beaten path. These can include hidden gems, unique cultural experiences, and outdoor adventures.

Consider visiting small towns and villages, exploring local markets, or taking part in a cultural workshop or class. You may also want to consider outdoor activities such as hiking, kayaking, or camping to get a closer look at Australia's natural beauty.

4. Ask locals for recommendations

One of the best ways to find off-the-beaten-path experiences is to ask

142

locals for recommendations. Locals can provide insider tips and recommendations that you may not find in guidebooks or online.

Strike up a conversation with locals at cafes, restaurants, or bars, and ask for their favorite activities and attractions in the area. You may also want to consider staying in a homestay or bed and breakfast, where you can interact with locals and get a more authentic experience.

5. Use technology to your advantage

Technology can be a valuable tool when it comes to finding the best activities and attractions. Use apps such as TripAdvisor, Google Maps, and Airbnb to research and book activities, and to find recommendations from other travelers.

You can also use social media to connect with locals and other travelers, and to find recommendations for off-the-beaten-path experiences. Follow local bloggers and influencers, and join travel groups to stay up-to-date on the latest travel trends and recommendations.

6. Be open to trying new things

Finally, the key to finding the best activities and attractions is to be open to trying new things. Travel is all about experiencing new cultures, trying new foods, and stepping out of your comfort zone.

Be open to trying new activities, exploring new neighborhoods, and meeting new people. You never know what amazing experiences you may discover when you're open to new opportunities.

Finding the best activities and attractions during your travels in Australia requires a combination of research, planning, and a willingness to step out of your comfort zone. By considering guided tours, off-the-beaten-path experiences, and asking locals for recommendations, you can create a memorable and fulfilling travel experience that will stay with you for the rest of your life.

## Chapter 6: Special Events and Festivals

Australia is a diverse and multicultural country that celebrates a variety of special events and festivals throughout the year. From cultural and religious celebrations to sporting events and music festivals, there is always something exciting happening in Australia. Here is an overview of some of the most popular special events and festivals in Australia.

1. Australia Day

Australia Day is celebrated on January 26th each year and commemorates the arrival of the First Fleet at Sydney Cove in 1788. The day is marked with parades, fireworks, concerts, and other festivities across the country. Many Australians also use the day to reflect on the nation's history and what it means to be Australian.

2. Sydney Gay and Lesbian Mardi Gras

The Sydney Gay and Lesbian Mardi Gras is an annual event that celebrates the LGBTQ+ community. The festival features a parade, parties, and events that promote diversity and inclusivity. The festival attracts thousands of visitors from around the world and is one of the largest LGBTQ+ events in the world.

3. Chinese New Year

Chinese New Year is celebrated in Australia with parades, dragon dances, and fireworks. The festival marks the beginning of the lunar new year and is a time for families to come together and celebrate. Many Chinese-Australians also celebrate with traditional foods and customs.

4. Melbourne Cup

The Melbourne Cup is Australia's premier horse racing event and is held annually on the first Tuesday in November. The event is known for its fashion and glamour, with attendees dressing up in their best outfits and hats. The race is also a public holiday in Victoria, and many Australians place bets on the horses.

5. Vivid Sydney

Vivid Sydney is a festival of light, music, and ideas that takes place in Sydney each year. The festival features light installations, music performances, and talks by leading thinkers and artists. The festival attracts visitors from around the world and has become one of Sydney's most popular events.

6. Dark Mofo

Dark Mofo is an annual winter festival that takes place in Hobart, Tasmania. The festival features art installations, music performances, and other events that explore the themes of darkness and light. The festival is known for its unconventional and provocative programming and attracts visitors from around the world.

## 7. Splendour in the Grass

Splendour in the Grass is one of Australia's largest music festivals and features a diverse lineup of international and local artists. The festival takes place over three days in Byron Bay and attracts thousands of music fans from around the country.

## 8. Adelaide Fringe

The Adelaide Fringe is an annual arts festival that takes place in Adelaide, South Australia. The festival features a diverse lineup of theatre, comedy, music, and other performances, as well as street performers and art installations. The festival is known for its inclusive and welcoming atmosphere and attracts visitors from around the world.

## 9. Melbourne International Comedy Festival

The Melbourne International Comedy Festival is one of the largest comedy festivals in the world and features a diverse lineup of local and international comedians. The festival takes place over several weeks in March and April and includes stand-up comedy, sketch comedy, and improv shows.

10. Byron Bay Bluesfest

The Byron Bay Bluesfest is a music festival that takes place over several days in Byron Bay, New South Wales. The festival features a lineup of blues, roots, and soul artists from around the world, as well as local acts. The festival is known for its relaxed atmosphere and attracts music fans from around the country.

Australia is home to a diverse range of special events and festivals that celebrate the country's culture, history, and creativity. From large-scale events to small local celebrations, there is something for everyone in Australia. Whether you're interested in music, art, sports, or culture, there is sure to be an event or festival that will pique your interest

## Communities to Know

Australia is a melting pot of cultures and communities, each with its unique history, traditions, and contributions to Australian society. From the Indigenous Australian communities to the various immigrant groups that have settled in Australia over the years, the country is home to a diverse range of communities. Here is an overview of some of the communities to know in Australia.

1. Indigenous Australians

Indigenous Australians are the original inhabitants of Australia and are believed to have lived on the continent for at least 60,000 years. There are over 250 distinct Indigenous Australian language groups, each with their unique cultural practices, beliefs, and traditions. The Indigenous Australian community has a rich cultural heritage and has made significant contributions to Australian society.

2. Chinese Australians

Chinese Australians have a long history in Australia, with the first Chinese immigrants arriving during the gold rush in the mid-1800s. Chinese Australians have made significant contributions to Australian society, particularly in the areas of food, business, and culture. Today, Chinese Australians make up one of the largest non-European migrant groups in Australia.

3. Greek Australians

Greek Australians have a strong presence in Australia, with the first Greek immigrants arriving in the country in the 1850s. Greek Australians have made significant contributions to Australian society, particularly in the areas of food, sport, and culture. Today, Greek Australians make up one of the largest ethnic groups in Australia.

4. Italian Australians

Italian Australians have a strong presence in Australia, with the first Italian immigrants arriving in the country in the 1880s. Italian Australians have made significant contributions to Australian society, particularly in the areas of food, wine, and culture. Today, Italian Australians make up one of the largest ethnic groups in Australia.

5. Vietnamese Australians

Vietnamese Australians have a significant presence in Australia, with the first Vietnamese immigrants arriving in the country in the 1970s. Vietnamese Australians have made significant contributions to Australian society, particularly in the areas of food, business, and culture. Today, Vietnamese Australians make up one of the largest non-European migrant groups in Australia.

6. Lebanese Australians

Lebanese Australians have a significant presence in Australia, with the first Lebanese immigrants arriving in the country in the 1880s. Lebanese Australians have made significant contributions to Australian society, particularly in the areas of food, business, and culture. Today, Lebanese Australians make up one of the largest ethnic groups in Australia.

7. Aboriginal and Torres Strait Islander Australians

Aboriginal and Torres Strait Islander Australians are the Indigenous peoples of Australia, with the Torres Strait Islander people living in the Torres Strait Islands between Australia and Papua New Guinea. The Aboriginal and Torres Strait Islander peoples have a rich cultural heritage and have made significant contributions to Australian society, particularly in the areas of art, music, and sport.

8. Muslim Australians

Muslim Australians have a significant presence in Australia, with the first Muslim immigrants arriving in the country in the 1860s. Muslim Australians have made significant contributions to Australian society, particularly in the areas of business, education, and culture. Today, Muslim Australians make up one of the largest religious groups in Australia.

9. Jewish Australians

Jewish Australians have a significant presence in Australia, with the first Jewish immigrants arriving in the country in the 1830s. Jewish Australians have made significant contributions to Australian society, particularly in the areas of education, business, and culture. Today, Jewish Australians make up one of the largest religious groups in Australia.

10. LGBT+ Australians

The LGBT+ community in Australia is diverse and vibrant, with significant contributions to Australian society, particularly in the areas of culture, arts, and activism. Australia has made significant progress in recent years in recognizing and protecting the rights of the LGBT+ community, including legalizing same-sex marriage in 2017.

Australia is a multicultural and diverse country, home to a range of communities with their unique history, traditions, and contributions to Australian society. From the Indigenous Australians to various immigrant groups, Australia has a rich cultural heritage, and exploring these communities can provide a unique insight into Australian culture and society. It is essential to approach these communities with respect and an open mind, recognizing the value and importance of their culture and contributions to Australia. By learning about and celebrating the diverse communities in Australia, we can promote understanding, tolerance, and respect for all cultures and people.

## **Best Museums and Art Galleries**

Australia is home to some of the best museums and art galleries in the world. These institutions showcase Australia's rich cultural heritage, diverse art scene, and natural history. From the National Gallery of Australia to the Museum of Old and New Art (MONA), there is something for every art and history lover in Australia. In this guide, we will explore some of the best museums and art galleries to visit in Australia.

1. National Gallery of Australia

The National Gallery of Australia (NGA) is located in Canberra and is the country's largest art museum. The gallery houses more than 160,000 works of art, including the largest collection of Australian art in the world. The NGA has an impressive collection of indigenous art, European art, and Asian art, as well as a sculpture garden. The museum also hosts temporary exhibitions throughout the year.

2. Museum of Old and New Art (MONA)

The Museum of Old and New Art (MONA) is located in Hobart, Tasmania and is one of the most unique and controversial museums in the world. The museum was founded by entrepreneur David Walsh and features a mix of ancient, modern, and contemporary art, as well as interactive installations and performance art. The museum's collection includes works by artists such as Sidney Nolan, Salvador Dali, and Damien Hirst. The museum also has a winery and a restaurant on the premises.

3. Australian Museum

The Australian Museum is located in Sydney and is the country's oldest museum. The museum has an extensive collection of natural history specimens, including animals, fossils, and minerals. The museum also has a large collection of indigenous artifacts, including tools, weapons, and art. The museum hosts temporary exhibitions and events throughout the year, as well as educational programs for all ages.

4. Art Gallery of New South Wales

The Art Gallery of New South Wales is located in Sydney and is one of the most visited art museums in Australia. The gallery has a collection of over 30,000 works of art, including

Australian art, European art, and Asian art. The museum's collection includes works by artists such as William Dobell, Arthur Streeton, and Brett Whiteley. The museum also hosts temporary exhibitions and events throughout the year.

5. National Museum of Australia

The National Museum of Australia is located in Canberra and is dedicated to showcasing Australia's social history and cultural heritage. The museum has a collection of over 210,000 objects, including indigenous artifacts, historic documents, and photographs. The museum also has interactive exhibits and multimedia displays that tell the story of Australia's history and culture.

6. Art Gallery of South Australia

The Art Gallery of South Australia is located in Adelaide and has a collection of over 45,000 works of art, including Australian art, European art, and Asian art. The museum's collection includes works by artists such as Claude Monet, Vincent van Gogh, and John Glover. The museum also hosts temporary exhibitions and events throughout the year.

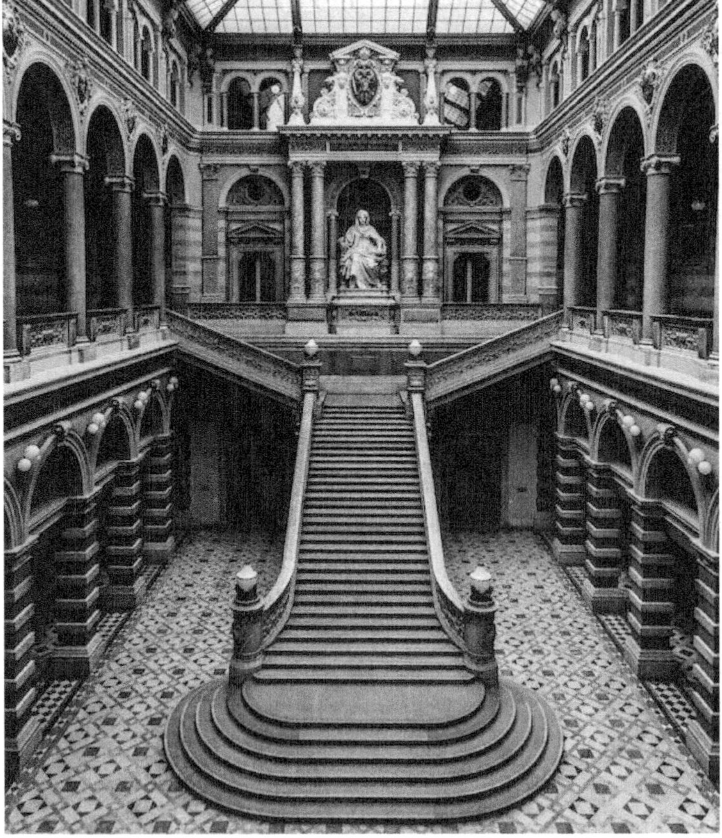

7. Western Australian Museum

   The Western Australian Museum is located in Perth and has a collection of over 4 million objects, including natural history specimens, cultural artifacts, and historic documents. The museum has several branches throughout the state, including the Maritime Museum and the WA Shipwrecks Museum. The museum also hosts temporary exhibitions and events throughout the year.

8. National Portrait Gallery

   The National Portrait Gallery is located in Canberra and is dedicated to showcasing portraits of significant Australians. The gallery has a collection of over 3,000 portraits, including paintings, photographs, and sculptures. The museum's collection includes portraits of prominent Australians such as Dame Edna

Everage, Rupert Murdoch, and Heath Ledger.

9. Museum and Art Gallery of the Northern Territory

The Museum and Art Gallery of the Northern Territory is located in Darwin and is dedicated to showcasing the natural and cultural history of the Northern Territory. The museum has a collection of over 1.2 million specimens, including fossils, plants, and animals. The museum also has a large collection of indigenous art and artifacts, including bark paintings, sculptures, and ceremonial objects. The museum hosts temporary exhibitions and events throughout the year, as well as educational programs for all ages.

10. Queensland Art Gallery and Gallery of Modern Art

The Queensland Art Gallery and Gallery of Modern Art (QAGOMA) is located in Brisbane and is one of the largest art museums in Australia. The museum has a collection of over 17,000 works of art, including Australian art, international art, and contemporary art. The museum's collection includes works by artists such as Pablo Picasso, Jackson Pollock, and Yayoi Kusama. The museum also hosts temporary exhibitions and events throughout the year.

11. National Film and Sound Archive

The National Film and Sound Archive is located in Canberra and is dedicated to preserving Australia's audiovisual heritage. The archive has a collection of over 3 million items, including films, television programs, music recordings, and sound effects. The archive also hosts screenings, exhibitions, and events throughout the year.

12. Museum of Contemporary Art Australia

The Museum of Contemporary Art Australia (MCA) is located in Sydney and is dedicated to showcasing contemporary art from Australia and around the world. The museum has a collection of over 4,000 works of art, including paintings, sculptures, and installations. The museum's collection includes works by artists such as Tracey Moffatt, Janet Laurence, and Yoko Ono. The museum also hosts temporary exhibitions and events throughout the year, as well as educational programs for all ages.

13. National Gallery of Victoria

The National Gallery of Victoria (NGV) is located in Melbourne and is the oldest and largest art museum in

Australia. The museum has a collection of over 70,000 works of art, including Australian art, European art, and Asian art. The museum's collection includes works by artists such as Rembrandt, Pablo Picasso, and Sidney Nolan. The museum also hosts temporary exhibitions and events throughout the year, as well as educational programs for all ages.

14. Bendigo Art Gallery

The Bendigo Art Gallery is located in Bendigo, Victoria and is one of the largest regional art galleries in Australia. The gallery has a collection of over 4,000 works of art, including Australian art, international art, and decorative arts. The museum's collection includes works by artists such as Fred Williams, Tom Roberts, and John Brack. The gallery also hosts temporary exhibitions and events throughout the year.

15. Heide Museum of Modern Art

The Heide Museum of Modern Art is located in Bulleen, Victoria and is dedicated to showcasing modern and contemporary art from Australia and around the world. The museum has a collection of over 6,000 works of art, including paintings, sculptures, and installations. The museum's collection includes works by artists such as Arthur Boyd, Albert Tucker, and Jenny Watson. The museum also hosts temporary exhibitions and events throughout the year, as well as educational programs for all ages.

Australia has a rich cultural heritage and diverse art scene, and its museums and art galleries are some of the best in the world. From the National Gallery of Australia to the Museum of Old and New Art (MONA), there is something for every art and history lover in Australia. These institutions showcase Australia's natural history, cultural heritage, and diverse art scene, and are must-visit destinations for anyone visiting the country.

## Chapter 7: Traveling with kids and families

Traveling with kids and families can be a rewarding experience, but it can also be challenging if not planned properly. Australia is a great destination for families, with a wide range of activities and attractions to suit all ages. In this guide, we'll provide tips and suggestions for traveling with kids and families in Australia.

1. Choose Family-Friendly Accommodation

When traveling with kids, it's important to choose family-friendly accommodation. Look for hotels and resorts that offer family rooms, cribs, high chairs, and other amenities for children. Many hotels also offer kids' clubs and activities to keep children entertained.

For a more affordable and authentic experience, consider staying in a vacation rental. Websites such as Airbnb and HomeAway offer a wide range of family-friendly accommodations, from apartments to villas.

2. Plan Age-Appropriate Activities

When planning your itinerary, consider the ages and interests of your children. Australia offers a wide range of activities and attractions for families, from theme parks to wildlife parks to museums. Here are some suggestions:

- For young children: Visit a zoo or wildlife park, such as Taronga Zoo in Sydney or the Lone Pine Koala Sanctuary in Brisbane. Take a scenic train ride, such as the Puffing Billy Railway in Victoria or the Kuranda Scenic Railway in Queensland. Visit a children's museum, such as the Powerhouse Museum in Sydney or the Questacon Science Museum in Canberra.
- For older children: Visit a theme park, such as Dreamworld in Queensland or Luna Park in Sydney. Go on a wildlife safari, such as the Great Ocean Road Wildlife Park in Victoria or the Kangaroo Island Wilderness Trail in South Australia. Take a surfing lesson, such as at Bondi Beach in Sydney or Surfers Paradise in Queensland.
- For the whole family: Visit a national park, such as the Blue Mountains National Park in New South Wales or the Great Barrier Reef Marine Park in

Queensland. Take a hot air balloon ride, such as in the Yarra Valley in Victoria or in the Hunter Valley in New South Wales. Visit a cultural attraction, such as the Aboriginal Cultural Centre and Keeping Place in New South Wales or the Museum of Old and New Art in Tasmania.

3. Pack Smart

When traveling with kids, it's important to pack smart. Bring along snacks, toys, books, and other items to keep your children entertained during long flights or car rides. Also, don't forget to pack sunscreen, insect repellent, and other essentials for outdoor activities.

If you're traveling with young children, consider bringing a stroller or baby carrier. Many attractions offer stroller rentals, but it's always best to bring your own to ensure comfort and familiarity for your child.

4. Use Public Transport

Using public transport can be a great way to get around with kids in Australia. Most cities have reliable and efficient public transport systems, including buses, trains, and trams. Many systems offer discounted fares for children, making it an affordable option for families.

5. Embrace the Outdoors

Australia is known for its beautiful outdoor landscapes and warm weather, making it the perfect destination for outdoor activities. From hiking to beach days to bike rides, there are plenty of outdoor activities to keep kids and families entertained.

Some popular outdoor activities for families include:

- Beach days: Australia has some of the most beautiful beaches in the world, with crystal clear waters and white sand. Popular beaches include Bondi Beach in Sydney, Surfers Paradise in

Queensland, and Cable Beach in Western Australia.
- Hiking: Australia has many national parks and hiking trails, offering scenic views and opportunities to spot wildlife. Popular hikes include the Royal National Park Coastal Walk in New South Wales, the Great Ocean Walk in Victoria, and the Larapinta Trail in the Northern Territory.
- Wildlife experiences: Australia is home to a diverse range of wildlife, and there are many opportunities for families to see and interact with animals. Some popular options include visiting wildlife sanctuaries and zoos, going on whale watching tours, and taking a trip to Kangaroo Island to see kangaroos, wallabies, and other native animals in their natural habitat.

Traveling with kids and families in Australia can be a rewarding and enjoyable experience with proper planning and research. From outdoor activities like beach days and wildlife experiences to indoor options like museums and theme parks, there are plenty of things to see and do that will keep both kids and adults entertained. It's important to consider factors like accommodation options, transportation, and budget when planning a family trip to Australia. Additionally, researching and booking family-friendly activities and tours ahead of time can help ensure a smooth and enjoyable vacation. With its natural beauty, vibrant culture, and friendly locals, Australia is a great destination for families looking for a fun and memorable vacation.

## **Kid-friendly attractions and activities**

Australia is a vast and beautiful country with a diverse range of attractions and activities that are perfect for kids of all ages. From the beaches and wildlife parks to theme parks and museums, there is no shortage of kid-friendly attractions and activities in Australia. In this guide, we will explore some of the best kid-friendly attractions and activities in Australia.

### 1. **Visit the Beaches**

Australia is known for its stunning beaches, and they are the perfect place for kids to enjoy some sun, sand, and sea. The country has a wide range of beaches to choose from, including family-friendly options with calm waters, patrolled beaches, and even those with playgrounds and BBQ areas.

Some of the best beaches for kids in Australia include:

- Bondi Beach, Sydney: This iconic beach is one of the most popular in the country, and it's a great place for kids to enjoy the waves, play in the sand, and enjoy the beachside playground.
- Surfers Paradise Beach, Gold Coast: This beach is perfect for kids who love to swim, and it also has a range of nearby attractions, including theme parks and wildlife parks.

- Manly Beach, Sydney: This family-friendly beach is great for kids of all ages, with calm waters and plenty of activities to keep them entertained.
- Noosa Main Beach, Sunshine Coast: This beach is great for families with young children, as it has shallow waters and a sheltered beach.
- Cable Beach, Broome: This stunning beach has crystal-clear waters and plenty of activities, including camel rides, making it a hit with kids.

## 2. Visit Wildlife Parks and Zoos

Australia is home to some of the most unique and fascinating wildlife in the world, and kids will love visiting the country's many wildlife parks and zoos. These attractions offer the opportunity to get up close and personal with native Australian animals, including kangaroos, koalas, wombats, and crocodiles.

Some of the best wildlife parks and zoos in Australia include:

- Taronga Zoo, Sydney: This zoo is one of the most famous in the country, and it's home to over 4,000 animals, including elephants, tigers, and gorillas.
- Australia Zoo, Sunshine Coast: This zoo was made famous by the late Steve Irwin, and it's a great place for kids to learn about and interact with native Australian wildlife, including crocodiles and koalas.

- Lone Pine Koala Sanctuary, Brisbane: This sanctuary is dedicated to koalas, and it's the perfect place for kids to get up close and personal with these adorable animals.
- Healesville Sanctuary, Melbourne: This sanctuary is located just outside Melbourne, and it's home to a range of native Australian animals, including kangaroos, wombats, and echidnas.
- Featherdale Wildlife Park, Sydney: This park is located just outside of Sydney, and it's home to over 1,700 animals, including wallabies, dingoes, and Tasmanian devils.

3. **Visit Theme Parks**

Australia is home to some of the best theme parks in the world, and they're a great place for kids to have some fun and excitement. These parks offer a range of rides, shows, and attractions that are sure to keep kids entertained for hours on end.

Some of the best theme parks in Australia include:

- Dreamworld, Gold Coast: This theme park is one of the biggest in the country, and it's home to a range of rides and attractions, including roller coasters, water rides, and animal exhibits.
- Warner Bros. Movie World, Gold Coast: This park is perfect for kids who love movies, and it's home to a range of movie-themed rides and attractions, including the Batman ride and the Scooby-Doo coaster.
- Sea World, Gold Coast: This park is perfect for kids who love marine animals, and it's home to a range of marine animal exhibits, as well as rides and attractions.
- Luna Park, Sydney: This historic amusement park is located in the heart of Sydney, and it's home to a range of classic rides, including the Ferris wheel and roller coaster.

- Adventure World, Perth: This park is located just outside of Perth, and it's home to a range of rides and attractions, including water slides, roller coasters, and a wildlife park.

## 4. Visit Museums

Australia has a rich history and culture, and visiting museums is a great way for kids to learn about the country's past and present. There are museums across the country that cater specifically to children, with interactive exhibits and hands-on activities that make learning fun.

Some of the best museums for kids in Australia include:

**Questacon, Canberra:** This science museum is perfect for kids who love to learn about how things work, with interactive exhibits that explore everything from gravity to electricity.

**Australian Museum, Sydney:** This museum is dedicated to natural history, with exhibits on dinosaurs, fossils, and Australian animals.

**National Museum of Australia, Canberra**: This museum explores the country's history and culture, with interactive exhibits that allow kids to learn about everything from Aboriginal culture to Australian democracy.

**Powerhouse Museum, Sydney:** This museum explores science and technology, with interactive exhibits that allow kids to experiment with everything from robots to flight simulators.

**Melbourne Museum, Melbourne:** This museum is dedicated to history and culture, with exhibits that explore everything from dinosaurs to the history of Melbourne.

5. Visit National Parks

Australia is home to some of the most beautiful and diverse natural landscapes in the world, and visiting national parks is a great way for kids to explore the great outdoors. There are national parks across the country that offer a range of activities, from hiking and camping to swimming and wildlife watching.

Some of the best national parks for kids in Australia include:

**Blue Mountains National Park, New South Wales:** This park is located just outside of Sydney, and it's home to stunning scenery, including waterfalls, cliffs, and forests.

**Uluru-Kata Tjuta National Park, Northern Territory:** This park is home to Uluru, one of the country's most iconic landmarks, as well as stunning rock formations and desert landscapes.

**Great Barrier Reef Marine Park, Queensland:** This park is perfect for kids who love marine animals, with opportunities for snorkeling, diving, and wildlife watching.

**Daintree National Park, Queensland**: This park is located in the tropical north of the country, and it's home to rainforests, beaches, and wildlife.

**Kakadu National Park, Northern Territory:** This park is home to stunning landscapes, including waterfalls, wetlands, and rugged escarpments, as well as a range of Aboriginal cultural sites.

Australia has a wide range of attractions and activities that are perfect for kids of all ages. From the beaches and wildlife parks to theme parks and museums, there is something for everyone to enjoy. So, whether you're planning a family vacation or just looking for something to do with the kids, be sure to check out some of these great kid-friendly attractions and activities in Australia.

## **Tips for traveling with children**

Traveling with children can be an incredibly rewarding experience, but it can also be challenging at times. Whether you're planning a road trip or a flight to a new destination, there are some tips and tricks that can help make your trip smoother and more enjoyable for everyone involved. Here are some tips for traveling with children:

1. Plan ahead

When traveling with children, it's important to plan ahead as much as possible. This includes booking flights or hotels well in advance, researching child-friendly activities in the area, and packing everything you need for the trip. It's also a good idea to create a loose itinerary for the trip, so you have an idea of what you'll be doing each day.

2. Pack smart

When packing for a trip with children, it's important to pack smart. This means bringing only the essentials and packing in a way that makes everything easy to access. It's also a good idea to pack a small carry-on bag with a change of clothes and some snacks in case of any unexpected delays or accidents.

3. Keep the kids entertained

One of the biggest challenges of traveling with children is keeping them entertained during long flights or car rides. To keep them occupied, pack some books, toys, or games that they enjoy. You can also download movies or TV shows on a tablet or smartphone to keep them entertained during the trip.

4. Take breaks

It's important to take breaks during long car rides or flights to allow the kids to stretch their legs and get some fresh air. Plan regular stops at rest areas or parks along the way, or take a break from the flight by walking up and down the aisle or doing some stretches in the back of the plane.

5. Be flexible

Traveling with children can be unpredictable, so it's important to be flexible and go with the flow. If your child is tired or cranky, take a break and let them rest. If your plans need to change due to unforeseen circumstances, be open to changing your itinerary to make the trip more enjoyable for everyone.

6. Involve the kids

One way to keep kids engaged and excited during a trip is to involve them in the planning process. Let them help choose activities or restaurants to visit, and give them a say in how the trip is structured. This can help them feel more invested in the trip and make it more enjoyable for everyone.

7. Be prepared for emergencies

No matter how well you plan, emergencies can happen when traveling with children. It's important to be prepared by packing a first aid kit, bringing any necessary medications, and having important phone numbers and documents on hand. You should also have a plan in case of any emergencies, such as a lost child or a medical issue.

8. Be mindful of schedules

When traveling with children, it's important to be mindful of their schedules, such as nap times or mealtimes. Try to plan activities around their schedules to avoid meltdowns or tantrums. You should also try to maintain their regular routines as much as possible to make the transition to a new environment easier.

9. Consider child-friendly accommodations

When booking accommodations, it's important to consider child-friendly options, such as hotels with swimming pools or playgrounds. You can also consider renting an apartment or house to give your family more space and flexibility during the trip.

10. Take advantage of child discounts

Many attractions and activities offer discounts for children, so be sure to take advantage of these opportunities. You can also look for family packages or deals that offer discounts for multiple people.

Traveling with children can be a challenging but rewarding experience. By planning ahead, packing smart, and being flexible, you can make your trip more enjoyable for everyone involved. With these tips in mind, you can create lasting memories with your family and explore new destinations together.

## Chapter 8: LGBTQ+ travel - suggestions for LGBTQ+ travelers, including accommodation, nightlife, and events.

Traveling as a member of the LGBTQ+ community can be an exciting and rewarding experience, but it can also come with unique challenges. In this guide, we will explore some tips and suggestions for LGBTQ+ travelers, including accommodation, nightlife, and events.

## Accommodation:

Finding LGBTQ+-friendly accommodation can be a challenge, especially in countries where homosexuality is not widely accepted or legal. However, there are a growing number of hotels and guesthouses that cater specifically to LGBTQ+ travelers. These establishments often provide a safe and welcoming environment for LGBTQ+ guests, with staff who understand the unique needs and concerns of the community.

When booking accommodation, look for places that explicitly advertise themselves as LGBTQ+-friendly, or that have high ratings on LGBTQ+ travel websites. Some popular websites that cater to LGBTQ+ travelers include GayTravel.com, Purple Roofs, and misterb&b. These websites can help you find LGBTQ+-friendly accommodation in a wide range of destinations, from major cities to rural areas.

**Nightlife:**

For many LGBTQ+ travelers, experiencing the local nightlife scene is an important part of the trip. Many cities have thriving LGBTQ+ nightlife scenes, with a wide range of bars, clubs, and other venues that cater specifically to the community.

When exploring the nightlife scene, it's important to prioritize your safety. Stick to well-lit and crowded areas, and avoid venturing into unfamiliar or unsafe neighborhoods. Be aware of your surroundings, and trust your instincts if something doesn't feel right.

If you're traveling alone, consider connecting with other LGBTQ+ travelers through social media or online forums. This can help you find like-minded people to explore the nightlife scene with, and can provide an added layer of safety.

**Events:**

Attending LGBTQ+ events can be a great way to connect with the local community and experience the culture of a destination. From pride parades to film festivals to art exhibits, there are a wide range of events that cater specifically to the LGBTQ+ community.

Before attending an event, do some research to ensure that it's safe and welcoming for LGBTQ+ travelers. Look for events that explicitly advertise themselves as

LGBTQ+-friendly, or that have high ratings on LGBTQ+ travel websites.

It's also important to be mindful of local customs and laws. In some countries, LGBTQ+ events may be illegal or frowned upon by the local community. Be respectful of local customs and laws, and prioritize your safety above all else.

**Destinations:**

There are many destinations around the world that are known for being LGBTQ+-friendly. Some popular destinations include:

1. Amsterdam, Netherlands: Amsterdam is known for its liberal attitudes and its thriving LGBTQ+ community. The city is home to a wide range of LGBTQ+-friendly bars, clubs, and other venues, and hosts a popular pride parade each year.
2. Berlin, Germany: Berlin is a popular destination for LGBTQ+ travelers,

with a vibrant nightlife scene and a wide range of LGBTQ+-friendly events and venues.
3. San Francisco, United States: San Francisco is known for its large LGBTQ+ community and its long history of activism. The city is home to a wide range of LGBTQ+-friendly businesses and organizations, and hosts a popular pride parade each year.
4. Bangkok, Thailand: Bangkok is known for its vibrant LGBTQ+ nightlife scene, with a wide range of bars, clubs, and other venues that cater specifically to the community.
5. Rio de Janeiro, Brazil: Rio de Janeiro is a popular destination for LGBTQ+ travelers, with a large and vibrant LGBTQ+ community. The city hosts a popular pride parade each year, and is home to a wide range of LGBTQ+-friendly businesses and organizations.

Here are some additional tips for LGBTQ+ travelers:

Research local laws and customs before traveling. In some countries, same-sex activity may be illegal or frowned upon by the local community. It's important to be aware of these laws and customs before traveling, and to prioritize your safety above all else.

Connect with other LGBTQ+ travelers online. Social media and online forums can be a great way to connect with other LGBTQ+ travelers and find recommendations for LGBTQ+-friendly accommodations, nightlife, and events.

Be mindful of public displays of affection. In some destinations, public displays of affection between same-sex couples may be frowned upon or even illegal. It's important to be mindful of local customs and laws, and to prioritize your safety above all else.

Consider a guided tour. Guided tours can be a great way to explore a destination while also prioritizing your safety as an LGBTQ+ traveler. There are a growing number of tour companies that cater specifically to LGBTQ+ travelers, and these tours can provide a safe and welcoming environment for exploring a destination.

Don't be afraid to ask for help. If you encounter any problems or feel unsafe while traveling, don't be afraid to ask for help. Many LGBTQ+-friendly accommodations, nightlife venues, and events have staff who are trained to assist LGBTQ+ travelers and provide a safe and welcoming environment.

LGBTQ+ travel can be an exciting and rewarding experience, but it's important to prioritize safety and find LGBTQ+-friendly accommodations, nightlife, and events. With the growing number of resources available to LGBTQ+ travelers, it's becoming easier to find safe and welcoming destinations around the world.

## Chapter 9: Shopping

Shopping in Australia is a unique and exciting experience, offering a diverse range of options from high-end luxury brands to local markets and everything in between. As a visitor to Australia, you will find an abundance of shopping opportunities, whether you are looking for souvenirs to take home or high-end designer goods. In this guide, we'll take a closer look at the world of shopping in Australia, including popular shopping destinations, unique Australian brands, and tips for making the most of your shopping experience.

## Popular Shopping Destinations

Australia has a wealth of shopping destinations, ranging from high-end luxury boutiques to outdoor markets. Here are some of the most popular shopping destinations to visit while in Australia:

1. Chadstone Shopping Centre - Located in Melbourne, Chadstone is the largest shopping centre in Australia and one of the largest in the Southern Hemisphere. It features over 500 stores, including high-end luxury brands such as Chanel, Gucci, and Prada.
2. Westfield Sydney - Located in the heart of Sydney, Westfield Sydney is a premier shopping destination featuring over 300 stores. It is home to many high-end luxury brands, as well as Australian fashion labels such as Zimmermann and Camilla and Marc.

3. Queen Victoria Building - Also located in Sydney, the Queen Victoria Building is a historic shopping centre that has been restored to its former grandeur. It features over 200 stores, including luxury brands such as Bvlgari and Dior, as well as local designers.
4. Melbourne Central - Located in Melbourne's CBD, Melbourne Central is a popular shopping destination featuring over 300 stores. It has a mix of high-end luxury brands, as well as Australian fashion labels such as Aje and Gorman.
5. Bondi Markets - Located in Sydney's iconic Bondi Beach, Bondi Markets is a popular outdoor market featuring over 100 stalls selling a variety of goods such as clothing, jewellery, and souvenirs.

## Unique Australian Brands

One of the great things about shopping in Australia is the abundance of unique and distinctive Australian brands. Here are some of the top Australian fashion brands to look out for while shopping:

1. Zimmermann - Known for its feminine and romantic designs, Zimmermann is a high-end fashion label that has gained global recognition. Founded in Sydney in 1991, the brand is known for its use of floral prints, delicate fabrics, and intricate details.
2. Aje - Founded in 2008, Aje is a contemporary fashion brand that combines Australian laid-back style with edgy, modern designs. The brand is known for its use of bold colours, voluminous silhouettes, and luxurious fabrics.
3. Gorman - Founded in 1999, Gorman is a quirky and colourful fashion label

that has become a staple of the Australian fashion scene. The brand is known for its bold prints, bright colours, and playful designs.
4. Camilla and Marc - Founded in 2003 by siblings Camilla and Marc Freeman, Camilla and Marc is a high-end fashion label that is known for its sophisticated and modern designs. The brand is known for its use of luxurious fabrics, clean lines, and understated elegance.
5. Bassike - Founded in 2006, Bassike is a minimalist fashion label that is focused on sustainable and ethical production. The brand is known for its use of organic cotton, relaxed silhouettes, and simple designs.

## **Tips for Making the Most of Your Shopping Experience**

Here are some tips to help you make the most of your shopping experience in Australia:

1. Check the exchange rate - Before you start shopping, check the exchange

rate to ensure that you are getting the best value for your money.

2. Look for tax-free shopping - Visitors to Australia may be eligible for tax-free shopping on purchases over a certain amount. Make sure to check with the retailer or ask for a tax refund form when making your purchase.

3. Research sales and discounts - Keep an eye out for sales and discounts, particularly during major shopping events such as Boxing Day (December 26th) or end of financial year sales (June 30th). Many retailers offer significant discounts during these periods.

4. Wear comfortable shoes - Shopping in Australia can involve a lot of walking, particularly if you are visiting a large shopping centre or outdoor market. Make sure to wear comfortable shoes to avoid sore feet.

5. Bring a reusable shopping bag - Many retailers in Australia have phased out

single-use plastic bags in favour of reusable shopping bags. Bringing your own reusable shopping bag is not only environmentally friendly, but it can also save you money as some retailers charge for bags.
6. Be aware of customs regulations - If you are purchasing goods to take back to your home country, be aware of customs regulations regarding imports. Some goods may be subject to restrictions or taxes upon entry to your home country.
7. Try local food and drink - Many shopping destinations in Australia feature local food and drink options, such as artisanal coffee shops or food halls. Trying local food and drink can be a great way to immerse yourself in the local culture while taking a break from shopping.

Shopping in Australia is a unique and diverse experience, offering everything from high-end luxury brands to local markets and unique Australian designers. By following these tips and doing a bit of research beforehand, you can make the most of your shopping experience while visiting Australia.

## **Overview of the local shopping scene in Australia, including markets, boutiques, and souvenir shops**

Australia offers a diverse and exciting shopping scene, with something to suit every taste and budget. From bustling markets to designer boutiques, and souvenir shops to artisanal goods, Australia's local shopping scene has it all. Here is an overview of some of the top shopping destinations in Australia.

**Markets:**

Markets are a staple of Australian shopping culture, offering everything from fresh produce to handmade crafts and vintage goods. Some of the most popular markets in Australia include:

1. Queen Victoria Market, Melbourne - One of the largest and oldest markets in Australia, Queen Victoria Market offers a wide variety of fresh produce, meat, seafood, and specialty products. It also features a range of fashion, homewares, and souvenir stalls.
2. The Rocks Markets, Sydney - Located in the historic Rocks precinct of Sydney, The Rocks Markets offer a range of artisanal goods, including jewelry, textiles, and artwork. There

are also food and drink stalls, making it a great place to sample local cuisine.
3. Salamanca Market, Hobart - Set against the backdrop of Hobart's historic Salamanca Place, Salamanca Market is Tasmania's most popular market. It features over 300 stalls selling everything from fresh produce to handmade crafts and clothing.
4. Mindil Beach Sunset Market, Darwin - This popular market in Darwin is held every Thursday and Sunday during the dry season (April to October) and features a range of food, craft, and souvenir stalls. It's also a great place to watch the sunset over the beach.

**Boutiques:**

Australia is home to many unique and stylish boutiques, offering everything from high-end designer fashion to niche vintage finds. Some of the top boutique destinations include:

1. Paddington, Sydney - Located just a few kilometers from the CBD, Paddington is a trendy suburb known for its designer boutiques and high-end fashion stores. It's the perfect place to shop for unique Australian fashion labels.
2. Chapel Street, Melbourne - One of Melbourne's most famous shopping precincts, Chapel Street is home to a range of fashion boutiques, vintage stores, and designer labels. It's also known for its eclectic mix of cafes and restaurants.
3. James Street, Brisbane - This trendy shopping precinct in Brisbane is home to a range of designer boutiques, homewares stores, and gourmet food shops. It's a great place to shop for unique gifts and souvenirs.
4. King William Road, Adelaide - This historic shopping district in Adelaide

features a range of designer boutiques, fashion stores, and gift shops. It's also known for its outdoor dining and relaxed atmosphere.

**Souvenir Shops:**

Australia is a popular destination for tourists, and as such, there are many souvenir shops offering a range of unique Australian gifts and mementos. Some of the top souvenir shops include:

1. Australian Way, Sydney - Located in Sydney's International Terminal, Australian Way offers a range of Australian gifts and souvenirs, including indigenous artwork, kangaroo leather products, and locally made chocolates.
2. Made in Australia, Melbourne - This boutique souvenir shop in Melbourne offers a range of locally made gifts, including clothing, jewelry, and

homewares. It's a great place to find unique Australian gifts.
3. Kakadu Australia, Cairns - This souvenir shop in Cairns offers a range of authentic Australian gifts, including boomerangs, didgeridoos, and indigenous artwork. It's the perfect place to find a unique Australian souvenir.
4. The Bowerbird Store, Adelaide - This boutique gift shop in Adelaide offers a range of locally made gifts, including homewares, jewelry, and children's toys. It's a great place to find unique and handmade gifts.

**Artisanal Goods:**

Australia is home to many talented artisans and makers, offering unique and handmade goods. Some of the top destinations for artisanal goods include:

1. The Finders Keepers Market - Held in Sydney, Melbourne, and Brisbane, The

Finders Keepers Market is a bi-annual event that showcases the work of over 200 independent designers and makers. It's the perfect place to shop for unique and handmade gifts.

2. Handmade Canberra - This bi-annual market in Canberra features over 260 Australian designers and makers, selling everything from ceramics to textiles and homewares. It's a great place to discover new and emerging Australian makers.
3. Fremantle Markets - Located in the historic port city of Fremantle in Western Australia, Fremantle Markets is a popular destination for handmade crafts, art, and food. It's been operating for over 100 years and is a must-visit for anyone in the area.
4. The Big Design Market - Held in Melbourne, Sydney, and Brisbane, The Big Design Market features over 250 stallholders selling design and handmade goods from across

Australia. It's the perfect place to shop for unique and one-of-a-kind gifts.

In addition to these top destinations, many Australian cities and towns have their own unique shopping scenes, featuring local artisans, designers, and makers. Whether you're looking for high-end fashion, handmade crafts, or unique souvenirs, Australia has something to offer everyone.

**Tips for Shopping in Australia:**

1. Check the opening hours - Many shops and markets in Australia have limited opening hours, particularly on weekends and public holidays. Make sure to check the opening hours before you go to avoid disappointment.
2. Be prepared for the weather - Australia's climate can be unpredictable, so it's a good idea to bring sunscreen, a hat, and an umbrella or rain jacket depending on the season.

3. Bring a reusable bag - Many shops and markets in Australia charge for plastic bags, so it's a good idea to bring a reusable bag or backpack to carry your purchases.
4. Check the return policy - Make sure to check the return policy before you make a purchase, particularly for high-end items. Some stores may not offer refunds or exchanges.
5. Look for tax-free shopping - Visitors to Australia may be eligible for tax-free shopping on purchases over a certain amount. Make sure to ask the retailer if they offer tax-free shopping and what the eligibility requirements are.
6. Bargain at markets - Many markets in Australia are open to bargaining, particularly for handmade or vintage items. Don't be afraid to negotiate with the seller for a better price.

Australia's local shopping scene offers a diverse range of options, from bustling markets to high-end boutiques and souvenir shops. Whether you're looking for handmade crafts, designer fashion, or unique souvenirs, there's something for everyone in Australia's shopping scene. Make sure to plan ahead, check the opening hours, and bring a reusable bag to make the most of your shopping experience in Australia.

## Tips on finding the best deals, haggling, and shopping locally

Australia has a vibrant shopping scene, with a wide range of options from luxury boutiques to flea markets. Here are some tips on finding the best deals, haggling, and shopping locally in Australia to save money on your purchases.

1. Research the Market

Before you start shopping, research the local market to get an idea of what the typical prices are for the items you're interested in. Use online resources, travel guides, and local forums to get an idea of the best places to shop and the going rates for different products.

2. Shop Local Markets

Local markets are a great place to find unique and locally made products, and they are often more affordable than shopping in a traditional retail store. In Sydney, head to Paddington Markets for handmade jewelry and clothing, while Melbourne's Queen Victoria Market offers fresh produce, handmade crafts, and souvenirs.

3. Look for Outlet Stores

Outlet stores are a great way to get designer clothing and accessories at a fraction of the retail price. Birkenhead Point Outlet Centre in Sydney offers discounts on brands such as Polo Ralph Lauren and Michael Kors, while DFO South Wharf in Melbourne has outlet stores for Nike, Tommy Hilfiger, and more.

### 4. Haggle at Markets

Many markets in Australia are open to haggling, especially for handmade or vintage items. Don't be afraid to negotiate with the seller for a better price, but make sure to be respectful and reasonable in your offers.

### 5. Use Discount Vouchers and Coupons

Many retailers in Australia offer discount vouchers and coupons that can be used to get discounts on your purchases. Check online coupon websites or sign up for retailer newsletters to get access to these offers.

### 6. Shop During Sales and Promotions

Look out for sales and promotions, especially during major holidays like Christmas and Easter. You can also find sales at the end of each season, when retailers are trying to clear out inventory to make room for new products.

## 7. Consider Secondhand Shopping

Secondhand stores and thrift shops can be a great way to find unique and affordable clothing and accessories. In Melbourne, try Retrostar Vintage Clothing for vintage clothing and accessories, while Sydney's Salvos Stores offer a wide range of secondhand products at affordable prices.

There are many ways to save money on shopping in Australia, from researching the market and shopping at local markets to using discount vouchers and coupons. By following these tips, you can get the best deals and make the most of your shopping experience in Australia.

## Chapter 10: Nightlife in Australia

Australia is known for its vibrant nightlife, with a wide range of options for locals and visitors alike. From trendy bars and clubs to live music venues and theater performances, there is something for everyone in Australia's nightlife scene. Here is an overview of the nightlife in Australia, including popular destinations and events.

### Bars and Clubs

Australia has a thriving bar and club scene, with many popular destinations in major cities like Sydney, Melbourne, and Brisbane. In Sydney, The Ivy is a popular rooftop bar and nightclub with a stunning view of the city skyline. In Melbourne, the Rooftop Bar and Cinema is a trendy spot with a rooftop cinema, bar, and lounge. Brisbane's Fortitude Valley is known for its bustling nightlife, with bars and clubs like The Met and The TBC Club.

**Live Music**

Australia is home to many talented musicians, and the country has a thriving live music scene. Major cities like Sydney, Melbourne, and Perth are known for their music festivals, including the Sydney Festival and Melbourne Music Week. Smaller venues like The Corner Hotel in Melbourne and The Enmore Theatre in Sydney host regular live music performances from local and international artists.

**Theater and Performances**

Australia is also known for its theater and performance scene, with many popular venues like the Sydney Opera House and the Arts Centre Melbourne. The Sydney Opera House hosts a wide range of performances, including opera, ballet, and theater, while the Arts Centre Melbourne is known for its live music, comedy, and dance performances.

## Festivals and Events

Australia hosts many festivals and events throughout the year, including cultural celebrations, music festivals, and sporting events. Some of the most popular events include the Sydney Gay and Lesbian Mardi Gras, the Melbourne Cup Carnival, and the Australian Open Tennis Tournament. The Vivid Sydney festival is also a major attraction, featuring light displays, music, and other performances throughout the city.

Australia's nightlife scene is diverse and vibrant, with many options for bars, clubs, live music, theater, and festivals. Whether you're looking for a trendy rooftop bar or a live music performance, there is something for everyone in Australia's nightlife.

## **Overview of the local nightlife scene in Australia, including bars, clubs, and live music venues**

Australia is known for its vibrant and diverse nightlife scene, with a plethora of options to cater to every taste and preference. From lively bars and clubs to intimate live music venues, Australia offers a range of experiences for locals and visitors alike. This guide provides an overview of the local nightlife scene in Australia, including popular bars, clubs, and live music venues.

**Bars**

Bars are a popular destination for those looking to enjoy a night out in Australia. With an abundance of trendy bars to choose from, it can be challenging to decide where to go. In Sydney, the Opera Bar offers spectacular views of the Opera House and Harbour Bridge. The Baxter Inn in Sydney is a hidden gem that offers a wide selection of whiskey, while the Lui Bar in Melbourne offers stunning views of the city skyline.

In Brisbane, the rooftop bar Eleven offers a panoramic view of the city, while the Gresham Bar offers a vintage atmosphere with a wide selection of cocktails. Perth's Mechanics Institute Bar offers a unique ambiance with a blend of industrial and vintage décor.

## Clubs

Australia is renowned for its energetic and diverse club scene, with a wide range of venues catering to different music genres and tastes. Home to some of the best nightclubs in the world, Australia offers a range of options for those looking to dance the night away.

In Sydney, the Marquee is a popular club located in The Star Casino that offers a range of music genres and celebrity appearances. The Ivy is another popular venue that offers multiple floors, a rooftop pool, and a range of music genres.

In Melbourne, the Chapel Street Precinct is home to some of the city's most popular clubs, including the infamous Revolver. The Night Cat in Fitzroy offers a range of music genres, including jazz, blues, and funk.

## Live Music Venues

Australia is known for its thriving live music scene, with many local and international artists performing at venues across the country. The Enmore Theatre in Sydney is a popular destination for live music, hosting local and international acts across a range of genres.

The Corner Hotel in Melbourne is another popular venue, hosting regular live music performances from local and international artists. The iconic Forum Theatre is a grand building that has played host to some of the biggest names in music, including Nirvana and Queen.

In Brisbane, the Fortitude Valley area is known for its lively live music scene. The Tivoli Theatre is a popular venue that hosts local and international artists, while The Triffid offers a range of music genres and a large outdoor area for performances.

In Perth, the Rosemount Hotel is a popular live music venue that has been operating for over 100 years. The Astor Theatre in Mount Lawley is another popular venue that hosts a range of music genres and other performances.

Australia's nightlife scene offers a diverse range of experiences for locals and visitors alike. Whether you're looking for a trendy bar or an energetic club, or want to enjoy live music performances, Australia has something to offer. With options available across major cities like Sydney, Melbourne, Brisbane, Perth, and more, Australia's nightlife scene is sure to impress.

## **Tips on finding the best places to go out, including recommendations for local bands and DJs**

Australia is home to a vibrant and diverse nightlife scene, with a range of options available for those looking to go out and enjoy themselves. However, finding the best places to go out can be a challenge, especially if you're not familiar with the local scene. This guide provides tips on finding the best places to go out in Australia, including recommendations for local bands and DJs.

## Research online

One of the best ways to find the best places to go out in Australia is to do your research online. There are many websites and social media pages dedicated to the local nightlife scene, which can provide you with valuable information on upcoming events, local bands, and DJs. Websites like Resident Advisor, Eventbrite, and Facebook Events are great resources for finding local events and performers.

In addition to these websites, many clubs and venues have their own social media pages that provide regular updates on upcoming events and performances. Following these pages can give you a better idea of what's happening in the local scene and help you find the best places to go out.

**Ask locals**

Another great way to find the best places to go out in Australia is to ask locals. Locals are often the best source of information on the local nightlife scene, as they are more likely to know about the latest events and venues. Whether you're staying in a hotel, Airbnb, or hostel, don't be afraid to ask the staff for recommendations on the best places to go out.

You can also ask locals you meet while out and about. Strike up a conversation with someone at a bar or club, and ask them for their recommendations on the best places to go out. You never know, you might make some new friends in the process!

## Explore different areas

Australia is a large and diverse country, with different cities and regions offering their own unique nightlife experiences. While major cities like Sydney, Melbourne, and Brisbane are well-known for their nightlife scenes, there are also many smaller cities and regional areas that offer a range of options for going out.

Exploring different areas can help you find hidden gems and discover new venues that you might not have otherwise known about. Whether you're visiting a new city or exploring the local area, be sure to venture out and explore different neighbourhoods to find the best places to go out.

## Attend local festivals and events

Australia is home to a range of local festivals and events, many of which offer a variety of music and entertainment options. Attending these events can be a great way to discover new bands and DJs, as well as meet like-minded people who share your interests.

Festivals like Splendour in the Grass, Falls Festival, and Laneway Festival are popular events that attract local and international performers. In addition to these larger festivals, many cities and towns host smaller events throughout the year, such as street festivals, cultural events, and food and wine festivals.

**Support local artists**

One of the best ways to discover new bands and DJs in Australia is to support local artists. Many bars, clubs, and live music venues feature local performers, giving you the opportunity to discover new talent and support the local music scene.

In addition to attending live performances, you can also find local artists online. Many local bands and DJs have their own websites and social media pages, where you can listen to their music and learn more about their upcoming performances.

Finding the best places to go out in Australia can be a challenge, but with a little bit of research and exploration, you can discover some hidden gems and have an unforgettable experience. Whether you're looking for the latest club scene or want to discover new local bands and DJs, Australia's nightlife scene has something to offer for everyone.

# Chapter 11: Practical Information

Practical information is essential for any visitor to Australia, as it can help you plan your trip and ensure that you have a safe and enjoyable experience. This guide provides some practical information on topics such as visas, currency, transportation, and communication in Australia.

## Visas

Visitors to Australia will generally require a visa to enter the country, depending on their nationality and the purpose of their visit. Some visitors may be eligible for a visa waiver, while others will need to apply for a visa before they travel. The most common types of visas for visitors to Australia include the Visitor visa, Working Holiday visa, and Student visa.

It's important to check the visa requirements for your specific nationality and circumstances, as they can vary depending on your country of origin and the length and purpose of your visit. You can find more information on visas and entry requirements on the Australian Government's Department of Home Affairs website.

**Currency**

The currency in Australia is the Australian dollar (AUD). Visitors can exchange their currency at banks, exchange offices, and some hotels and airports. ATMs are also widely available throughout the country, and most major credit cards are accepted.

It's a good idea to check the exchange rate before you travel, so that you can get a better idea of how much your money is worth in Australian dollars. You can also use online currency converters to help you plan your budget.

## Transportation

Australia is a large country, and transportation options can vary depending on where you are and where you want to go. Some popular transportation options for visitors include:

- Domestic flights: Australia has a well-developed domestic airline network, with flights operating between major cities and regional areas.
- Trains: The train network in Australia is limited compared to some other countries, but there are some scenic train journeys available, such as the Ghan and the Indian Pacific.
- Buses: Buses are a popular option for travel within cities and between regional areas.
- Taxis and ride-sharing services: Taxis and ride-sharing services like Uber are widely available in cities and regional areas.

It's a good idea to research transportation options before you travel, so that you can plan your itinerary and budget accordingly.

**Communication**

Australia has a good telecommunications network, with mobile phone coverage available in most urban and regional areas. Visitors can purchase SIM cards from mobile phone providers like Telstra, Optus, and Vodafone, which can be used in unlocked mobile phones.

In addition to mobile phone coverage, there are also many public Wi-Fi hotspots available throughout the country, including in cafes, hotels, and airports. However, it's important to be cautious when using public Wi-Fi, as it can be less secure than private networks.

**Emergency services**

In case of emergency, visitors can call the following numbers:

- Police, fire, and ambulance: 000
- Non-emergency police assistance: 131 444
- Lifeline (24-hour crisis support and suicide prevention): 13 11 14

It's a good idea to familiarize yourself with these numbers before you travel, so that you know who to call in case of an emergency.

Australia is a beautiful and diverse country, with plenty to offer visitors from around the world. By following these practical tips, you can ensure that your trip to Australia is safe, enjoyable, and memorable.

**Tips on staying safe and healthy while traveling in Australia , including information on local laws and customs, medical facilities, and emergency resources**

Australia is a safe and welcoming country, but like any destination, visitors should take precautions to stay safe and healthy while traveling. This guide provides some tips on how to stay safe and healthy in Australia, including information on local laws and customs, medical facilities, and emergency resources.

1. Familiarize yourself with local laws and customs

Australia has strict laws on issues such as drug use, drinking and driving, and animal welfare. Visitors should familiarize themselves with local laws and customs to avoid getting into legal trouble. For example, in many parts of Australia, it is illegal to smoke in public places or to bring tobacco products into the country.

Additionally, Australia has a unique culture and way of life, and visitors should be respectful of local customs and traditions. For example, it is important to respect Indigenous cultural sites and to ask permission before taking photographs.

2. Take precautions against the sun and heat

Australia is known for its warm weather and sunny skies, but this can also pose a health risk for visitors who are not used to the climate. To stay safe and healthy, it is important to take precautions against the sun and heat, such as wearing sunscreen, a hat, and sunglasses, and staying hydrated.

In addition, visitors should be aware of the risks of heat stroke and other heat-related illnesses, especially during the summer months. If you start to feel dizzy, nauseous, or fatigued, it is important to seek shade and stay hydrated.

3. Use caution when swimming

Australia is home to some of the world's most beautiful beaches and swimming spots, but visitors should take caution when swimming in the ocean or in natural bodies of water. The ocean can be unpredictable and dangerous, with strong currents and rip tides that can quickly sweep swimmers out to sea.

Visitors should always swim between the red and yellow flags on patrolled beaches, which indicate safe swimming areas. Additionally, it is important to avoid swimming alone or after dark, and to be aware of any warnings or signs posted at the beach.

4. Seek medical attention if necessary

Australia has a high standard of medical care, with modern hospitals and medical facilities located throughout the country. However, medical care can be expensive, especially for visitors who are not covered by the Australian health care system.

It is important to purchase travel insurance before you travel to Australia, which can help cover the cost of medical care in case of illness or injury. Additionally, visitors should be aware of the location of medical facilities in the areas they are traveling to, and should seek medical attention if they experience any symptoms or health issues.

5. Know where to find emergency resources

In case of emergency, visitors can call the following numbers:

- Police, fire, and ambulance: 000
- Non-emergency police assistance: 131 444
- Lifeline (24-hour crisis support and suicide prevention): 13 11 14

It is important to familiarize yourself with these numbers before you travel, so that you know who to call in case of an emergency. Additionally, visitors should be aware of the location of emergency services and medical facilities in the areas they are traveling to.

6. Be aware of wildlife hazards

Australia is home to a diverse array of wildlife, including many species that can pose a hazard to humans. Visitors should be aware of the risks posed by snakes, spiders, and other animals, and should take precautions to avoid them.

For example, visitors should wear closed-toe shoes and long pants when hiking in areas where snakes are common, and should be cautious when reaching into crevices or other hidden areas. Additionally, visitors should be aware of the risks posed by jellyfish and other marine life when swimming in the ocean.

7. Take precautions against crime

Australia is a safe country overall, but visitors should take precautions against crime just like in any other country.

Here are some tips to help you stay safe:

1. Avoid isolated areas: When traveling in unfamiliar areas, stick to well-lit and populated areas. Avoid alleys, parks, and other isolated areas, especially at night.

2. Keep your valuables safe: Keep your valuables, such as your passport, money, and credit cards, in a safe place. Carry only what you need for the day, and leave the rest in a hotel safe or a secure location.
3. Be aware of pickpockets: Pickpocketing is a common crime in tourist areas. Keep an eye on your belongings and be aware of your surroundings.
4. Watch your drinks: Be cautious of accepting drinks from strangers, and never leave your drink unattended. Drink spiking is a serious issue in Australia, and can result in robbery, sexual assault, or other crimes.
5. Use licensed taxis: Always use licensed taxis, and make sure the driver uses the meter. Avoid unmarked taxis, and never get into a car with a driver who approaches you on the street.
6. Use common sense: Use common sense and trust your instincts. If a

situation feels unsafe, leave immediately.
7. Learn about the local laws: Laws and customs can vary between different states and territories in Australia. For example, smoking is banned in enclosed public spaces in some states, and it is illegal to drink alcohol in public places in some areas. Be aware of local laws and customs to avoid any trouble with authorities.

Traveling to Australia can be a great experience, with plenty of sights to see and things to do. However, it is important to take precautions to ensure your safety and health while in the country. By following these tips, you can enjoy your trip to Australia with peace of mind.

# Information on visas, travel insurance, and other practical matters

Traveling to another country requires careful planning, and there are several practical matters to consider before embarking on your journey. Here's some important information on visas, travel insurance, and other practical matters to help you prepare for your trip.

## Visas

Most visitors to Australia require a visa. The type of visa you need will depend on the purpose of your visit, the length of your stay, and your country of citizenship. Here are the main types of visas available:

1. Visitor visa: This visa allows you to visit Australia for tourism, visiting friends or family, or other non-work purposes. It can be valid for up to 12 months, but the length of stay is usually limited to 3 months per visit.

2. Working holiday visa: This visa is available to young people aged 18 to 30 from eligible countries, and allows you to work and travel in Australia for up to 12 months.
3. Student visa: If you plan to study in Australia for more than 3 months, you will need a student visa.

To apply for a visa, visit the Australian Government's Department of Home Affairs website. Make sure you apply well in advance of your trip, as processing times can vary.

**Travel insurance**

Travel insurance is an important consideration when traveling overseas. It can provide coverage for unexpected events such as medical emergencies, trip cancellations, lost or stolen luggage, and more. Here are some tips to help you choose the right travel insurance for your trip:

1. Look for comprehensive coverage: Make sure your travel insurance covers all the things you need, such as medical emergencies, trip cancellations, and lost or stolen luggage.
2. Compare policies: Shop around to find the best policy for your needs and budget. You can compare policies online or use a travel insurance broker.
3. Read the fine print: Before you purchase travel insurance, make sure you understand the policy's coverage, limitations, and exclusions.
4. Declare any pre-existing conditions: If you have any pre-existing medical conditions, make sure you declare them to your insurer. Failure to do so could invalidate your coverage.

**Other practical matters**

Here are some other practical matters to consider before your trip to Australia:

1. Currency: The currency in Australia is the Australian dollar (AUD). You can exchange currency at banks, exchange bureaus, and some hotels and airports.
2. Electrical outlets: The electrical outlets in Australia are Type I, which require a two- or three-pronged plug. Make sure you bring a converter if your devices use a different type of plug.
3. Time zone: Australia has three time zones: Australian Eastern Standard Time (AEST), Australian Central Standard Time (ACST), and Australian Western Standard Time (AWST).
4. Emergency services: In case of an emergency, dial 000 to reach the ambulance, police, or fire brigade. This call is free from any phone.

Traveling to Australia can be a rewarding experience, but it requires careful planning and preparation. Make sure you research the visa requirements for your trip, purchase travel insurance, and consider other practical matters before your departure. With proper planning, you can enjoy a safe and hassle-free trip to Australia.

## **Tips for a successful and enjoyable trip**

Australia is a vast and diverse country with many unique attractions and experiences to offer visitors. Whether you are planning a short trip or an extended stay, here are some tips to help you have a successful and enjoyable trip to Australia.

1. Plan ahead One of the most important things you can do to ensure a successful trip to Australia is to plan ahead. This includes researching your destination, booking accommodation and activities in advance, and creating an itinerary that includes all the sights and experiences you want to have.
2. Know the climate Australia has a diverse climate, so it's important to

research the weather conditions in the area you will be visiting. This will help you pack appropriately and plan your activities accordingly.
3. Pack wisely When packing for your trip to Australia, make sure to bring comfortable shoes, sunscreen, insect repellent, and a hat to protect you from the sun. You may also want to pack a light jacket or sweater for cooler evenings, as well as a swimsuit and beach towel if you plan to spend time at the beach.
4. Get travel insurance Travel insurance is an important consideration for any trip, and Australia is no exception. Make sure to get comprehensive travel insurance that covers medical expenses, trip cancellations, and any other unexpected events that may arise during your trip.
5. Be respectful of local customs Australia is a multicultural country with many unique customs and

traditions. To avoid causing offense or misunderstandings, it's important to research and respect local customs and etiquette.
6. Use public transportation Australia has a well-developed public transportation system, including buses, trains, and ferries. Using public transportation is not only an environmentally friendly option, but it can also be a more cost-effective and convenient way to get around.
7. Try local cuisine Australia is famous for its diverse and delicious cuisine, and trying local dishes is a must-do for any visitor. From seafood to meat pies, vegemite to pavlova, there is something for everyone to enjoy.
8. Stay connected Staying connected while traveling in Australia is important for safety and convenience. Consider getting a local SIM card or using a mobile hotspot to stay connected to the internet, as well as

keeping important contacts and emergency numbers on hand.
9. Be prepared for outdoor activities Australia is known for its beautiful outdoor spaces, including beaches, forests, and national parks. If you plan to engage in outdoor activities, make sure to bring appropriate gear and clothing, as well as plenty of water and snacks.
10. Have fun! Finally, the most important tip for a successful and enjoyable trip to Australia is to have fun! With so much to see and do, it's easy to get caught up in the planning and logistics of your trip. Remember to relax, take in the sights, and enjoy your time in this beautiful and welcoming country.

## Respecting the local culture and environment

Respecting the local culture and environment is important for any traveler, and Australia is no exception. The continent is home to a rich and diverse culture, as well as unique ecosystems and wildlife that should be treated with care and respect. Here are some tips for respecting the local culture and environment while traveling in Australia:

1. Learn about the local culture: Take the time to learn about the history, customs, and traditions of the Indigenous peoples of Australia, who have lived on the continent for thousands of years. This can include visiting cultural centers, participating in traditional activities, and engaging with the local communities.
2. Respect sacred sites: Many sites across Australia are considered sacred to Indigenous peoples, including Uluru

(also known as Ayers Rock) and Kata Tjuta (also known as the Olgas). Visitors should show respect and follow any guidelines or restrictions in place for visiting these sites.
3. Practice responsible tourism: Be mindful of your impact on the environment and local communities. This can include minimizing your use of plastic, respecting wildlife and their habitats, and supporting local businesses and tour operators.
4. Follow local laws and customs: Be aware of the laws and customs of the area you are visiting, and follow them accordingly. This can include respecting dress codes, not drinking in public, and obeying traffic laws.
5. Be mindful of cultural appropriation: Avoid appropriating cultural traditions or symbols without permission or understanding of their meaning. This includes wearing Indigenous cultural dress or using

cultural artifacts without permission or understanding of their significance.
6. Respect wildlife and their habitats: Australia is home to many unique and endangered species of wildlife, and it is important to treat them with respect and care. This can include not feeding or touching wild animals, and staying on designated paths and trails to avoid damaging their habitats.
7. Support conservation efforts: There are many organizations and initiatives working to protect the environment and wildlife in Australia. Consider supporting these efforts through donations, volunteering, or eco-friendly tourism activities.

By respecting the local culture and environment, travelers can have a more meaningful and enjoyable experience in Australia, while also contributing to the preservation of the continent's unique heritage and ecosystems.

## **Staying safe and healthy**

Staying safe and healthy while traveling in Australia is important for a successful and enjoyable trip. Here are some tips to help ensure your safety and well-being:

1. Get travel insurance: It is highly recommended to obtain travel insurance before embarking on any trip to Australia. This will provide coverage for medical emergencies, trip cancellations, and other unforeseen events.
2. Be aware of local dangers: Australia is known for its diverse and sometimes dangerous wildlife, including snakes, spiders, and sharks. Be aware of the risks and take necessary precautions, such as staying on designated paths and wearing protective clothing.
3. Follow beach safety guidelines: Australia has many beautiful beaches,

but they can also be dangerous. Follow beach safety guidelines, such as swimming only between the flags, and never swim alone.
4. Drink responsibly: Australia has a drinking culture, but it is important to drink responsibly to avoid accidents or incidents. Plan transportation in advance, and never drink and drive.
5. Protect yourself from the sun: Australia has a high level of UV radiation, which can cause sunburn and skin damage. Wear protective clothing and sunscreen with a high SPF.
6. Stay hydrated: Australia can have high temperatures and dry climates, so it is important to drink plenty of water to avoid dehydration.
7. Know emergency numbers: In case of an emergency, know the local emergency numbers and keep them handy.

8. Follow local laws and customs: Be aware of the laws and customs of the area you are visiting, and follow them accordingly. This can include respecting dress codes, not drinking in public, and obeying traffic laws.
9. Be aware of your surroundings: Stay aware of your surroundings and avoid walking alone at night in unfamiliar areas.
10. Seek medical attention if needed: If you experience any health issues while traveling in Australia, seek medical attention promptly.

By following these tips, travelers can enjoy a safe and healthy trip to Australia. It is also recommended to consult with a healthcare professional before traveling to ensure that you are up-to-date on necessary vaccinations and to discuss any specific health concerns you may have.

## Common Scams to Avoid

While Australia is generally a safe and honest country, there are still some scams that tourists should be aware of in order to avoid being a victim of fraud. Here are some of the most common scams to watch out for:

1. Fake tickets or tours: Be wary of buying tickets or tours from unofficial sources, especially on the street. Scammers may offer counterfeit tickets or tours that are not legitimate, leaving you with no entry or no refund.
2. Credit card fraud: Always keep an eye on your credit card and be careful when giving your credit card information over the phone or online. Also, be cautious of ATM machines, particularly if they are in isolated or dimly lit areas.
3. Overcharging: Be sure to check prices and ask about additional fees before agreeing to anything. Some vendors

may overcharge tourists or add extra fees for seemingly no reason.
4. Fake charities: Beware of individuals who approach you asking for donations for a charity. Always research the charity and make sure it is legitimate before donating.
5. Street hustlers: Street hustlers may try to lure tourists into a game or bet, claiming they can win money. These games are usually rigged, and tourists can end up losing a lot of money.
6. Rental car scams: Always read the fine print when renting a car to ensure you understand all the fees and conditions. Some rental car companies may try to add extra fees or insurance that you do not need.
7. Accommodation scams: Be wary of advertisements for accommodation that seem too good to be true. Always research the property and read reviews before making a booking, and never pay in advance without

confirming the booking with the property.

By being aware of these scams and exercising caution when dealing with unfamiliar situations or individuals, tourists can avoid becoming victims of fraud and enjoy a safe and hassle-free trip to Australia.

## **Dealing with unexpected situations**

Even with the best planning and preparation, unexpected situations can arise during a trip to Australia. Here are some tips for dealing with unexpected situations:

1. Stay calm: It can be easy to panic when unexpected situations arise, but it is important to stay calm and think logically about how to handle the situation.
2. Seek help: If you find yourself in a difficult situation, don't hesitate to seek help. Whether it's from hotel staff, local authorities, or fellow

travelers, there are usually people who can assist you.
3. Have backup plans: It is always a good idea to have backup plans in case of unexpected situations. For example, having copies of important documents stored electronically in case the physical copies are lost or stolen.
4. Stay informed: Keep up to date on current events and potential hazards, such as natural disasters or political unrest. This can help you make informed decisions about your travel plans.
5. Take precautions: While Australia is a generally safe country, it is still important to take precautions to protect yourself and your belongings. This might include avoiding certain areas at night, keeping valuables out of sight, and being aware of your surroundings.
6. Have travel insurance: Travel insurance can provide peace of mind

in case of unexpected situations, such as medical emergencies or trip cancellations. Be sure to research and purchase a policy that covers your specific needs.

By staying calm, seeking help when needed, having backup plans, staying informed, taking precautions, and having travel insurance, tourists can better handle unexpected situations and continue to enjoy their trip to Australia.

## Chapter 12: Itineraries

Australia is a vast country with diverse landscapes and experiences to offer. Planning a trip can be overwhelming, especially if you want to see as much as possible. Here are some suggested itineraries to help you plan your trip:

1. The Classic East Coast Tour: This itinerary covers the major cities and attractions along the eastern coast of Australia. Start in Sydney and spend a few days exploring the city, including the iconic Opera House and Harbour Bridge. From there, head north to the beautiful beaches of Byron Bay and the Gold Coast. Continue up to Brisbane, where you can explore the city and nearby attractions such as the Lone Pine Koala Sanctuary. Next, head to Cairns to explore the Great Barrier Reef and the Daintree Rainforest. Finish off the trip in Melbourne, where you can experience

the city's vibrant culture and food scene.
2. The Outback Adventure: For those looking to explore the rugged and remote interior of Australia, this itinerary is for you. Start in Alice Springs and explore the surrounding desert landscapes, including Uluru (Ayers Rock) and Kata Tjuta (the Olgas). From there, head north to Darwin, where you can explore Kakadu National Park and Litchfield National Park. Then, head west to Broome, where you can relax on the beautiful Cable Beach and explore the Kimberley region. Finish off the trip in Perth, where you can explore the city's beaches and nearby attractions such as Rottnest Island.
3. The Great Ocean Road Trip: This itinerary takes you along the stunning coastline of Victoria. Start in Melbourne and head south along the Great Ocean Road, stopping to see the

Twelve Apostles and other iconic rock formations along the way. Continue along the coast to the charming seaside towns of Port Fairy and Warrnambool. From there, head inland to the Grampians National Park, where you can hike and explore the beautiful landscapes. Finish off the trip back in Melbourne, where you can experience the city's food, culture, and nightlife.

4. The Tropical North Queensland Adventure: This itinerary takes you to the beautiful tropical region of North Queensland. Start in Cairns and explore the Great Barrier Reef and the Daintree Rainforest. From there, head north to Cape Tribulation and the beautiful beaches of the far north coast. Then, head inland to the Atherton Tablelands, where you can explore the waterfalls and rainforest. Finish off the trip in Port Douglas, where you can relax on the beach and

explore the nearby attractions such as Mossman Gorge.

No matter which itinerary you choose, be sure to take your time and soak up all that Australia has to offer. Remember that Australia is a vast country, and it's impossible to see everything in one trip. Plan ahead, prioritize the places and experiences that are most important to you, and be prepared to be flexible and adapt to unexpected situations.

**Suggested itineraries for different lengths of stay and interests, including options for solo travelers, families, and couples.**

Australia is a vast country with a variety of experiences and destinations to offer travelers. Whether you are a solo traveler, a family, or a couple, there is something for everyone in Australia. In this guide, we will provide suggested itineraries for different lengths of stay and interests.

**Short Trips (3-5 Days)**

If you only have a few days to explore Australia, we recommend focusing on one city or region. Here are some ideas:

Sydney:

Day 1: Explore the iconic sights of Sydney, including the Opera House and Harbour Bridge.

Day 2: Visit the famous Bondi Beach and take a coastal walk to Coogee Beach.

Day 3: Take a day trip to the Blue Mountains National Park to experience stunning views and natural beauty.

Melbourne:

Day 1: Visit the Royal Botanic Gardens and explore the trendy neighborhoods of Fitzroy and Collingwood.

Day 2: Take a day trip to the Great Ocean Road to see the Twelve Apostles and other natural wonders.

Day 3: Explore the famous laneways of Melbourne and try some of the city's famous coffee and food.

Brisbane:

Day 1: Visit South Bank and enjoy the cultural precinct, including the Queensland Museum and Gallery of Modern Art.

Day 2: Take a day trip to the famous Australia Zoo or the Lone Pine Koala Sanctuary.

Day 3: Visit the Gold Coast for a day of theme parks, beach, and shopping.

Perth:

Day 1: Take a walk through Kings Park and explore the city center.

Day 2: Visit the famous Fremantle Markets and take a tour of the Fremantle Prison.

Day 3: Take a day trip to Rottnest Island to see the famous Quokkas and experience the natural beauty of the island.

**Longer Trips (7-10 Days)**

If you have more time to explore Australia, we recommend visiting multiple cities and regions to experience the diverse landscapes and cultures. Here are some ideas:

Sydney - Melbourne - Great Ocean Road - Adelaide:

Day 1-3: Explore the iconic sights of Sydney and take a day trip to the Blue Mountains National Park.

Day 4-5: Visit Melbourne and explore the trendy neighborhoods and famous laneways. Day 6: Drive the Great Ocean Road and see the Twelve Apostles and other natural wonders.

Day 7-8: Visit Adelaide and explore the famous Barossa Valley wine region.

Day 9-10: Visit Kangaroo Island to see the native wildlife and natural beauty.

Cairns - Port Douglas - Great Barrier Reef - Daintree Rainforest:

Day 1-3: Explore Cairns and visit the Great Barrier Reef for a day of snorkeling or diving.

Day 4-5: Visit Port Douglas and explore the beautiful beaches and tropical rainforest.

Day 6-7: Take a guided tour of the Daintree Rainforest and experience the natural beauty and unique wildlife.

Day 8-10: Relax in the luxurious resorts of Palm Cove and enjoy the stunning views of the Coral Sea.

Darwin - Kakadu National Park - Litchfield National Park:

Day 1-3: Explore Darwin and visit the famous Mindil Beach Sunset Market.

Day 4-5: Take a guided tour of Kakadu National Park to experience the stunning landscapes and native wildlife.

Day 6-7: Visit Litchfield National Park and swim in the natural swimming holes and waterfalls.

Day 8-10: Take a day trip to the Tiwi Islands to experience the unique Aboriginal culture and art.

## 2-Week Itinerary for Families

Day 1-3: Sydney - Explore the city's iconic attractions like the Opera House, Harbour Bridge, and Bondi Beach. Take the kids to the Taronga Zoo or SEA LIFE Sydney Aquarium, and visit the Royal Botanic Garden for a picnic and a view of the city skyline.

Day 4-6: Blue Mountains - Drive west to the stunning Blue Mountains region, where you can go hiking, rock climbing, or take a scenic cable car ride. Visit the Jenolan Caves or take a trip on the Zig Zag Railway.

Day 7-10: Gold Coast - Fly to the Gold Coast for some fun in the sun. Visit the theme parks like Dreamworld, Warner Bros. Movie World, and Wet'n'Wild, or hit the beach for some surfing lessons.

Day 11-13: Cairns and the Great Barrier Reef - Fly to Cairns and take a tour of the Great Barrier Reef. Snorkel or scuba dive among the colorful coral and marine life, and take a scenic helicopter tour for a bird's eye view of the reef.

Day 14: Departure - Fly back to Sydney for your departure flight.

**2-Week Itinerary for Couples**

Day 1-4: Sydney - Explore the city's iconic attractions like the Opera House, Harbour

Bridge, and Bondi Beach. Take a sunset harbor cruise, enjoy a romantic dinner at a waterfront restaurant, and visit the Royal Botanic Garden for a picnic and a view of the city skyline.

Day 5-6: Hunter Valley - Drive north to the Hunter Valley wine region for a romantic getaway. Take a wine tasting tour, hot air balloon ride, or visit the Hunter Valley Gardens.

Day 7-10: Great Ocean Road - Fly to Melbourne and take a scenic drive along the Great Ocean Road. Visit the Twelve Apostles rock formations, the Otway National Park, and the charming coastal towns along the way.

Day 11-13: Kangaroo Island - Fly to Adelaide and take a ferry to Kangaroo Island for a secluded island getaway. Visit the wildlife sanctuaries, go hiking or kayaking, and enjoy the pristine beaches.

Day 14: Departure - Fly back to Sydney for your departure flight.

**1-Week Itinerary for Solo Travelers**

Day 1-3: Melbourne - Explore the city's trendy neighborhoods like Fitzroy, St. Kilda, and Brunswick. Visit the National Gallery of Victoria, the Melbourne Museum, and the Queen Victoria Market for some shopping.

Day 4-5: Great Ocean Road - Take a day tour from Melbourne to the Great Ocean Road to see the Twelve Apostles and other natural wonders.

Day 6-7: Sydney - Fly to Sydney for a few days of exploring the city's iconic attractions like the Opera House, Harbour Bridge, and Bondi Beach. Take a sunset harbor cruise or visit the Royal Botanic Garden for a picnic and a view of the city skyline.

**5-Day Family Itinerary**

Day 1: Sydney

- Visit the iconic Sydney Opera House and take a tour of the venue.
- Enjoy a family picnic in the Royal Botanic Garden and take a walk around the park.
- Head to Darling Harbour for dinner and entertainment, including a visit to the SEA LIFE Sydney Aquarium.

Day 2: Sydney

- Take a day trip to the Blue Mountains National Park and enjoy a scenic hike or take the scenic railway.
- Visit the Featherdale Wildlife Park to see native Australian wildlife, including koalas and kangaroos.

Day 3: Gold Coast

- Take a flight to the Gold Coast and spend the day exploring the beaches and water activities.
- Visit the Dreamworld amusement park and enjoy the thrill rides and shows.

Day 4: Gold Coast

- Visit the Currumbin Wildlife Sanctuary to learn about and interact with native Australian animals.
- Take a hike in the Tamborine Mountain National Park and enjoy the views.

Day 5: Gold Coast

- Visit the Warner Bros. Movie World amusement park and enjoy the themed rides and shows.
- Spend the afternoon at Surfers Paradise Beach and enjoy the sunset.

**7-Day Couples Itinerary**

Day 1: Sydney

- Take a walk around the city and explore the historic district, including The Rocks and Circular Quay.
- Enjoy a sunset cruise on the Sydney Harbour.

Day 2: Sydney

- Visit the Art Gallery of New South Wales and explore the local art scene.
- Take a ferry to Manly Beach and enjoy the laid-back vibe of the beachside town.

Day 3: Sydney

- Take a day trip to the Hunter Valley wine region and enjoy a wine tasting tour.
- Enjoy a romantic dinner at a local restaurant.

Day 4: Melbourne

- Take a flight to Melbourne and spend the day exploring the city, including the Federation Square and the Melbourne Museum.
- Enjoy a dinner at a local restaurant and sample the local cuisine.

Day 5: Melbourne

- Take a day trip to the Great Ocean Road and enjoy the scenic drive along the coast.
- Visit the Twelve Apostles and enjoy the views of the rock formations.

Day 6: Melbourne

- Visit the Yarra Valley wine region and enjoy a wine tasting tour.
- Take a hot air balloon ride over the vineyards at sunrise.

Day 7: Melbourne

- Take a walk around the Royal Botanic Gardens and enjoy the views of the city skyline.
- Visit the Crown Casino and enjoy the entertainment and dining options.

**14-Day Itinerary for Solo Travelers:**

Day 1-3: Explore Sydney's iconic landmarks and attractions such as the Opera House, Harbour Bridge, and Taronga Zoo.

Day 4-5: Take a day trip to the Blue Mountains and explore the stunning natural scenery.

Day 6-7: Fly to Melbourne and spend the next few days exploring the city's culture, food, and nightlife. Visit the Royal Botanic Gardens, the National Gallery of Victoria, and the Queen Victoria Market.

Day 8: Take a day trip to the Yarra Valley wine region for a day of wine tasting and indulging in delicious food.

Day 9-10: Fly to Uluru and explore the stunning Uluru-Kata Tjuta National Park. Take a guided tour to learn about the indigenous culture and history.

Day 11-12: Fly to Adelaide and explore the city's vibrant food and wine scene. Visit the Adelaide Central Market, the South Australian Museum, and the Art Gallery of South Australia.

Day 13-14: Fly to Tasmania and explore the island's natural beauty and wildlife. Visit the Freycinet National Park, the Cradle Mountain-Lake St. Clair National Park, and the Tasmanian Devil Unzoo.

These itineraries are just a starting point, and you can customize them according to your interests and preferences. Whether you're traveling solo, with your family, or with your partner, Australia offers a wealth of experiences and attractions that are sure to make your trip unforgettable.

## **The thing you should not miss**

Here are some things you should not miss when visiting Australia:

1. Experience the Great Barrier Reef

The Great Barrier Reef is the world's largest coral reef system and one of the most diverse ecosystems on the planet. It spans over 2,300 kilometers along the coast of Queensland and is home to thousands of species of marine life, including whales, dolphins, sea turtles, and over 1,500 species of fish. The best way to experience the Great Barrier Reef is by taking a boat tour or snorkeling or diving to explore the colorful coral formations and the marine life.

2. Visit Uluru

Uluru, also known as Ayers Rock, is a sacred site of the indigenous Anangu people and one of Australia's most iconic landmarks. This massive sandstone rock formation is located in the heart of the Australian Outback and is a popular destination for tourists. Visitors can take a guided tour to learn about the local culture and history or watch the sunrise or sunset over Uluru, which is a breathtaking sight.

3. Explore the Australian Outback

The Australian Outback is a vast, arid region that covers most of the country's interior. It is a unique and beautiful landscape that is home to a variety of wildlife and is steeped in indigenous culture and history. Visitors can explore the Outback by taking a guided tour or a self-drive trip, where they can visit iconic destinations such as Uluru, Kata Tjuta, and Kings Canyon, or go on a safari to spot kangaroos, wallabies, and other wildlife.

4. Go on a road trip along the Great Ocean Road

The Great Ocean Road is a scenic coastal drive that spans over 240 kilometers along the southern coast of Victoria. It is one of Australia's most popular road trips and offers stunning views of the coastline, rugged cliffs, and sandy beaches. Visitors can stop at iconic landmarks such as the Twelve Apostles, London Bridge, and Loch Ard Gorge, or go hiking in the nearby national parks.

5. Visit the wine regions

Australia is renowned for its wine, and there are several wine regions that visitors can explore. The most famous of these regions are the Barossa Valley in South Australia, the Hunter Valley in New South Wales, and the Yarra Valley in Victoria. Visitors can take a guided tour to learn about the wine-making process, sample some of the local varieties, and enjoy a gourmet meal paired with the perfect wine.

6. Enjoy the beaches

Australia is known for its beautiful beaches, and there are plenty to choose from. Some of the most popular beaches include Bondi Beach in Sydney, Surfers Paradise on the Gold Coast, and Cable Beach in Broome. Visitors can enjoy swimming, sunbathing, surfing, or just relaxing on the beach with a good book.

7. Visit the cities

Australia's cities are vibrant, multicultural, and offer a range of attractions and activities. Some of the most popular cities to visit include Sydney, Melbourne, Brisbane,

Perth, and Adelaide. Visitors can explore the city's landmarks, museums, art galleries, and entertainment venues, or enjoy the local food and nightlife scene.

Overall, Australia offers a wealth of attractions and experiences for visitors to enjoy. Whether you are interested in wildlife, nature, culture, history, food, or adventure, there is something for everyone. By planning your itinerary carefully and taking the time to explore the country's diverse regions and attractions, you can make your trip to Australia a truly unforgettable experience.

**Making the most of your trip**

Australia is a vast and diverse country with so much to offer, and making the most of your trip requires some careful planning and consideration. Here are some tips on how to make the most of your time in Australia:

1. Prioritize your must-see destinations: Australia is a huge country, and it's impossible to see everything in one trip. Before you go, make a list of your must-see destinations and prioritize them according to your interests and available time. This will help you make the most of your time and ensure that you don't miss out on anything important.
2. Take advantage of local knowledge: One of the best ways to get the most out of your trip to Australia is to take advantage of local knowledge. Speak to locals, tour guides, and other travelers to get recommendations on the best places to eat, drink, and visit.
3. Try new things: Australia is a country of many cultures, and there are plenty of opportunities to try new things. Whether it's trying kangaroo or crocodile meat, surfing, or experiencing Aboriginal culture, be open to new experiences and take

advantage of the unique opportunities available to you.
4. Plan your activities ahead of time: Australia has so many activities and attractions, and it can be overwhelming to try and do everything. Plan your activities ahead of time to ensure that you make the most of your time and budget. Many popular attractions, such as Uluru and the Great Barrier Reef, require advance bookings.
5. Consider a tour or package: If you're short on time or overwhelmed by the options, consider booking a tour or package. There are many tour operators that offer packages that include accommodation, transportation, and activities, making it easy to see the highlights of Australia in a short amount of time.
6. Take advantage of free activities: Australia has plenty of free activities to offer, from hiking to beaches to

museums. Take advantage of these opportunities to save money and experience the country in a more authentic way.
7. Stay connected: Australia is a modern country with excellent internet and mobile coverage. Stay connected to keep in touch with loved ones, plan your activities, and stay up to date on local events and news.

By following these tips, you can make the most of your trip to Australia and create memories that will last a lifetime.

## **Final thoughts and next steps**

Planning and executing a successful trip to any destination requires a bit of research and preparation. Australia is a unique and diverse country that offers a wide range of experiences for travelers. With its stunning landscapes, bustling cities, and rich culture, it is no surprise that Australia is a popular destination for travelers from all over the world.

To make the most of your trip to Australia, it is important to plan ahead and research your options. This guide has provided tips and suggestions for everything from transportation and accommodations to activities and local customs. By following these tips and doing your own research, you can ensure a successful and enjoyable trip to Australia.

In addition to planning ahead, it is also important to stay open-minded and flexible during your travels. Sometimes unexpected situations may arise, and it is important to be able to adapt and adjust your plans accordingly. Embrace the local culture and try new things, whether it be food, activities, or ways of life.

One of the best ways to enhance your travel experience is to connect with locals and other travelers. Australia is known for its friendly and welcoming people, so take the opportunity to make new friends and learn about their experiences and perspectives. This can also lead to new discoveries and hidden gems that you may not have found on your own.

As a final step, don't forget to document your trip and share your experiences with others. Whether it be through social media, a travel journal, or simply sharing stories with friends and family, reflecting on your trip can help solidify your memories and inspire others to embark on their own adventures.

In summary, planning and executing a successful trip to Australia requires a combination of research, flexibility, and open-mindedness. By following the tips and suggestions outlined in this guide, you can ensure a memorable and enjoyable trip to this unique and diverse country. So start planning, pack your bags, and get ready for an unforgettable adventure in Australia!

## Most frequently asked questions and answers about visiting Australia

Q: Do I need a visa to visit Australia?

A: Yes, most visitors need a visa to enter Australia. You can apply for a visa online, and the type of visa you need will depend on the purpose and length of your stay.

Q: What is the best time of year to visit Australia?

A: The best time of year to visit Australia depends on your interests and which parts of the country you plan to visit. Generally, the best time to visit is during the Australian summer (December-February), but keep in mind that this is peak tourist season.

Q: What are some must-see destinations in Australia?

A: Some must-see destinations in Australia include the Great Barrier Reef, Sydney Opera House, Uluru, the Great Ocean Road, and the Daintree Rainforest.

Q: Is it safe to travel in Australia?

A: Yes, Australia is generally a safe country to travel in. However, it's always important to take precautions to ensure your safety and security.

Q: What is the local currency in Australia?

A: The local currency in Australia is the Australian dollar (AUD).

Q: What is the drinking age in Australia?

A: The legal drinking age in Australia is 18 years old.

Q: What is the voltage in Australia?

A: The voltage in Australia is 240V, and the power outlets are different from those in other countries, so you may need an adapter.

Q: What is the time difference between Australia and other countries?

A: The time difference between Australia and other countries varies depending on which part of the country you are in and which time zone you are in. Generally, Australia is ahead of most other countries, with Sydney being 10-11 hours ahead of London and 14-16 hours ahead of New York.

Q: What is the best way to get around Australia?

A: The best way to get around Australia depends on your itinerary and budget. Some popular options include renting a car, taking public transportation, or flying between destinations.

Q: Is it safe to swim at Australian beaches?

A: Yes, it is generally safe to swim at Australian beaches. However, it is important to pay attention to warning signs about strong currents, rips, and dangerous marine life such as sharks and jellyfish. Always swim between the red and yellow flags, which mark the safest areas on the beach.

Q: Are there any dangerous animals in Australia?

A: Yes, there are some dangerous animals in Australia, such as snakes, spiders, crocodiles, and sharks. However, these animals are rarely encountered by visitors who follow basic safety precautions, such as staying on marked trails, not swimming in unpatrolled areas, and avoiding touching or approaching wildlife.

Q: Are there any cultural customs or etiquette I should be aware of when visiting Australia?

A: Yes, there are a few cultural customs and etiquette tips to keep in mind when visiting Australia. For example, it is considered impolite to arrive more than 15 minutes late for a social engagement, and it is customary to bring a small gift, such as a bottle of wine or chocolates, when invited to someone's home. Australians also tend to use informal language and enjoy a relaxed, casual style of conversation.

Q: Can I use my mobile phone in Australia?

A: Yes, most mobile phones from around the world will work in Australia, but you may need to check with your provider about international roaming fees. Alternatively, you can purchase a local SIM card or use a mobile hotspot.

Q: What is the tipping etiquette in Australia?

A: Tipping is not generally expected in Australia, but it is appreciated for exceptional service. If you do choose to tip, a 10% tip is considered generous.

Q: Can I drive in Australia with my foreign driver's license?

A: Visitors to Australia can drive with their foreign driver's license as long as it is in English or has an official translation. If your license is not in English, you will need to obtain an International Driving Permit.

**Australia Survival Phrases**

Australia is a beautiful and diverse country with a unique culture, language, and customs. While most Australians speak English, there are still a few phrases that can help visitors navigate daily life, communicate effectively, and show respect for the local culture. In this guide, we will provide some essential survival phrases to help you during your visit to Australia.

1. Greetings and Introductions

Greeting someone in Australia is typically done with a smile and a friendly "hello" or "hi." However, using a few additional phrases can help establish a connection and show your interest in the local culture.

- G'day: This is a classic Australian greeting that means "hello" or "good day." It's a casual and friendly way to greet someone and is commonly used throughout the country.
- How's it going? / How ya doin'? / How are you?: These phrases are all used as a way to ask someone how they are doing or to start a conversation.
- My name is...: If you are introducing yourself, you can use the phrase "My name is..." followed by your name.

2. Ordering Food and Drinks

Australia has a vibrant food and drink culture, with a wide range of options available. If you're dining out, these phrases can help you order what you want and make sure your dietary needs are met.

- I'm vegetarian / vegan / gluten-free: If you have specific dietary requirements, it's important to let your server know. These phrases can help ensure that your food is prepared to your specifications.
- Could I have... / I'd like...: These are polite ways to ask for what you want when ordering food or drinks.
- Cheers! / Bottoms up!: These phrases are commonly used when toasting or drinking with friends.

3. Getting Around

Australia is a large country, and getting around can be a challenge for visitors. These phrases can help you navigate public transportation, taxis, and other modes of travel.

- How do I get to...?: If you need directions or help finding your way, this phrase can be used to ask for assistance.
- How much is it?: When using public transportation or taking a taxi, it's important to know how much you will be charged. This phrase can help you clarify the cost.
- Can you take me to...?: If you're taking a taxi, this is a polite way to ask the driver to take you to your destination.

4. General Phrases

These phrases can be used in a variety of situations, from asking for help to expressing gratitude.

- Excuse me: This is a polite way to get someone's attention or to ask for help.

- Thank you: It's always important to express gratitude when someone helps you or provides a service.
- Sorry: If you make a mistake or accidentally bump into someone, saying "sorry" is a polite way to apologize.
- Goodbye: When it's time to say goodbye, you can use the phrase "goodbye" or "see you later."

Learning these essential phrases can help you communicate effectively and respectfully during your visit to Australia. Don't be afraid to practice them with locals and other visitors - you never know where a simple greeting or conversation starter may lead!

Printed in Great Britain
by Amazon